D0945225

After Words

After Words

Ron Mehl

Multnomah® Publishers *Sisters, Oregon*

AFTER WORDS
published by Multnomah Publishers, Inc.

© 2006 by Joyce C. Mehl, Trustee, Joyce C. Mehl Revocable Living Trust
International Standard Book Number: 1-59052-626-0

Unless otherwise indicated, Scripture quotations are from:
The Holy Bible, New King James Version © 1984 by Thomas Nelson, Inc.
Other Scripture quotations are from:
New American Standard Bible (NASB) © 1960, 1977 by the Lockman Foundation
The Holy Bible, New International Version (NIV) © 1973, 1984 by International Bible
Society, used by permission of Zondervan Publishing House
The Living Bible (TLB) © 1971.
Used by permission of Tyndale House Publishers, Inc. All rights reserved.
Holy Bible, New Living Translation (NLT)
© 1996. Used by permission of Tyndale House Publishers, Inc. All rights reserved.
The Holy Bible, King James Version (KJV)
The New Testament in Modern English, Revised Edition (Phillips)
© 1958, 1960, 1972 by J. B. Phillips

Multnomah is a trademark of Multnomah Publishers, Inc.,
and is registered in the U.S. Patent and Trademark Office.
The colophon is a trademark of Multnomah Publishers, Inc.

Printed in China

For information:
MULTNOMAH PUBLISHERS, INC. • 601 N LARCH STREET • SISTERS, OR 97759

Library of Congress Cataloging-in-Publication Data
Mehl, Ron.
After words / Ron Mehl.
p. cm.
ISBN 1-59052-626-0
1. Christian life. 2. Conduct of life. I. Title.
BV4501.3.M445 2006
248.4—dc22

2005029229

06 07 08 09 10—10 9 8 7 6 5 4 3 2 1 0

Dealing with Sin

Concluding Thoughts

Foreword

People knew my dad, Ron Mehl, for many reasons.

Many knew him from the simple yet profound sermons he delivered from the pulpit for more than thirty years. Others recognized his voice from his long-running radio program. In the latter season of his life, even more people across the nation loved him for the encouraging books that he wrote.

But way back in 1986, before he was what I would jokingly refer to as a "real" published writer, he wrote and assembled two copies of a little red leather-bound book which he entitled *Father Knows Best*. This is the book that—through evolution and revision—would eventually become what you now hold in your hands.

Only two copies of the original version were ever produced. One for me, and one for my brother, Mark. Mine sits proudly on my family room mantel and is perhaps my most prized earthly possession. I know that Mark, with his similar yet personalized-for-him version, feels the same.

Not long ago, I asked my brother what this book has meant to him. He had two thoughts. In light of the fact that Dad went to be with the Lord in 2003, Mark said that he is truly thankful to have a tangible, personal, written record of Dad's beliefs, interpretations, and advice. There have been times when, faced with an important life decision, he wondered, *What would Dad have said about this?* At other times, searching for insight into what the Lord meant in a given passage in the Bible—or maybe just needing reassurance that he's making the right decision for the right reasons—having a resource like this little book is truly a gift from God.

And Mark added something else. Having lived with Dad and seen firsthand the blood, sweat, and tears that go into writing a book like this, he knows that it was no small undertaking. In a world inhabited by many fathers whose lives are marked by so much selfishness, who are so disconnected from or even uninterested in their children's lives that they rarely have time for them, Mark believes it is both incredible and humbling to have a dad who would take time out of such a crazy schedule just to put this "little red book" together for us. It is truly a testament of our dad's love and devotion to his sons.

For me personally, this book arrived at a critical juncture in my life. I was headed off to a college three thousand miles from home, and I didn't know a soul on the entire eastern seaboard. Like my brother, I definitely felt blessed to have a tangible resource to turn to whenever I really needed to hear from my dad but wasn't able to speak with him directly.

Looking back on that time, however, I have to admit that I didn't really appreciate it as much as I might have. My dad had been battling leukemia for six years or so at that point, but it had yet to advance. In my young eyes, he really didn't look that much worse for wear. An invincible father. I believed God was going to heal him, or at the very least let him carry on indefinitely, stricken with his illness in a "Paul-like" way.

And carry on he did, for a long time. The longer he remained strong, the more I took for granted that he'd always be there. But eventually, to my surprise, the Lord called him home at age fifty-nine.

Now that my dad has gone to be with the Lord, this book has taken on new meaning for me. Where I once believed he would always be there for me, I now find myself having landed squarely in that category of people I once felt deep sorrow for—those who, for whatever reason, whether it be neglect, abandonment, estrangement, or death, don't have an earthly father in their lives to turn to in times of need.

I'm not a dad yet myself, so it makes me sorry to think that my children will never know their grandfather. Even so, I'm thankful that I will have the knowledge and wisdom in this book to draw upon, and that when they're of age, they too will be able to read my "little red book" and have a model of a godly father to look to.

And so, even as Mark and I revisit these pages when it's decision making time or when we need encouragement, we want to share this very personal part of our dad with all of you. Whether you are a young man looking for fatherly advice, or a father yourself looking for the Word's perspective on what your role should be to your own children, hear the words of a man who truly walked with the Lord, and truly loved his sons.

Ron Mehl Jr.
Mark Mehl
September 2005

Introductory

The Story of a Father's Book

I've always said that the most meaningful book I ever wrote had a very short print run.

Two copies.

The two copies went to the two young men I care about more than any young men on the face of the planet: my two sons, Ron Jr. and Mark. I gave them each a copy when they graduated from high school. It was a book that listed critical life concerns—personal convictions very close to this dad's heart.

You might not think so, but the task of putting that original little book together was no small chore. It represented many months of study, reflection, prayer, work—and a lifetime of experience. Joyce and I actually printed it ourselves and found a bookbinder in north Portland who lovingly bound it in leather, then hand stamped on each cover the title *Father Knows Best* in gold lettering.

Why did I do that? Why did I take the trouble as a father to write such things to my sons? Why did I have the books typeset and printed and bound? Because I wanted the book packaged in such a way that Ron and Mark could take and keep it with them over the long haul. I wanted to ensure that if they were ever confused or troubled in their minds, or wondered what their dad might think or do in a given situation, they would at least have *something* to turn to. I wanted them to realize through the years that I cared enough about them and their future to capture my heart for them in words on a page.

As I wrote, I felt as though I was pouring out my life for my sons, knowing that my time with them under our roof was short. I knew they would soon be independent young men, out on their own in the wide world.

And now they are gone. Both married. Both with homes of their own. In fact, this last December our first granddaughter, Liesl, was born.

Many who have heard me speak of that little volume, *Father Knows Best*, asked if they could have a copy. Dads and moms wanted it for their own children. Young men and women who miss a dad's love and guidance wanted it for themselves.

But I had a problem.

When I gave those volumes to Ron and Mark, I promised them that the words inside were just for them—father to son—and that I would never publish those thoughts.

I've kept that promise. With the exception of a couple of short pieces, the book you hold in your hands is all new material. But the idea is still the same…and so is the heart. I have written these pages as though I am writing to those boys of mine, and now to their children as well. And I really am. These are all thoughts and concerns and reminders I would like very much to pass along to my sons, my grandchildren…and to young men and women everywhere.

There are young men and women in our flock here in Beaverton who face disappointments, dangers, incredible pressures, and confusing crossroads, and don't know which way to turn. As their pastor, I wish I could be there for them. All of them. I wish I could impart some word of encouragement or warning or blessing that might point them toward God's eternal Word and the Savior who loves them so deeply.

Beyond our church's walls, countless other young men and women find themselves at profound turning points. Some wonder whether the Christian life is really worth it. Others contemplate disastrous shortcuts. Many wonder if anyone really cares. A few contemplate whether life itself is even worthwhile.

I wish I could be there for them too.

I would say to all of them what I would say to my own sons: Here are a few things you might want to consider, might want to take to heart, might want to keep handy…for the times when I can't be there.

First Thoughts

But the path of the righteous is like the light of dawn,

that shines brighter and brighter until the full day.

PROVERBS 4:18, NASB

It seems like yesterday that I was standing in the hospital gazing at a small bundle with a red and wrinkled face. When the nurse pointed through the window and said, "That one's yours!" I had no concept of the joy and blessing you would bring to our lives.

Had I known, I might not have been so filled with fear.

What kind of fear? You'll understand someday, Son. And you'll feel it, too, when your children grow up.

- *Fear that an amateur dad like me might let you down.*
- *Fear that I might fail to do my part in helping you become the man God intended you to be from the foundations of the earth.*

- *Fear that I might fail to impart the purpose and destiny that are yours as a man created in God's image.*
- *Fear that I might not prepare you adequately for the day you leave my home to establish a home of your own.*

And now, that "leaving home" time is closer than I like to think about. When the day comes, your mother and I will certainly have mixed feelings. On the one hand, we think everyone in the world should be privileged to know you as we have known you. But oh, Son...how we will miss you! You can't even imagine...until, perhaps, you have a son or daughter of your own.

Walk through any bookstore and you'll pass shelves filled with books about great men and women. These are people who have offered notable contributions to society, made great scientific discoveries, established or altered philosophical views, and, in some instances, even redirected the course of nations.

I'm not concerned about whether a book is written about me. I wouldn't want to waste the paper and ink. Do you know why?

Because *you* are my book, Son.

As Paul said:

You yourselves are our letter, written on
our hearts, known and read by everybody.
You show that you are a letter from Christ,
the result of our ministry, written not with
ink but with the Spirit of the living God,
not on tablets of stone but on tablets of
human hearts. (2 Corinthians 3:2–3, NIV)

It's one thing to impress people from a distance.
That's the easy part. That's exterior, surface stuff.
Over the last few years I've had the opportunity to
write some books, speak at some large conferences,
and stand before a few television cameras — things I'd
never imagined myself doing in my earlier years.

It's not that difficult to make an initial, superficial
impression. It's not so very hard to dress sharp, shine
your shoes, say nice things, and leave people thinking
you're a pretty impressive guy.

That's the easy part.

What *is* difficult is actually living your life before
someone, up close, day after day, in every situation.
That's where the true and lasting impressions are
made. And how I pray that my life, as I've lived it

before you, has been written across the pages of your heart.

Little of what I write in this little book will be new to a bright, intelligent young person like you. You've probably heard me say most of these things before. As Solomon put it, there's nothing new under the sun. But I think Peter said it best when he told us we could all stand a little reminding now and then.

> I plan to keep on reminding you of these
> things even though you already know them
> and are really getting along quite well!... As
> long as I am still here I intend to keep send-
> ing these reminders to you, hoping to
> impress them so clearly upon you that you
> will remember them long after I have gone.
> (2 Peter 1:12, 14–15, TLB)

My desire is that this collection of thoughts might give you a little boost in your confidence in those moments when you have to make a tough decision in a confusing situation or under pressing circumstances. I hope it may also raise a flag of caution at times, prompting you to seek the Lord's face with even more intensity.

The further you walk into life, the more you will discover that opportunities come equipped with hard choices. As your father, I have been just as concerned through the years about how you make your decisions as I have the decisions themselves.

In these pages, I will be sharing some of my own experiences and observations about the way life works—as well as some of my desires for your life and future. But when all is said and done, I don't want you to be making decisions just because "Dad said so." I don't want you to simply conform to the expectations of others; I want you to make decisions on the basis of convictions in your own heart and life.

When you come to those perplexing forks in the road, you need to have a *process* by which you arrive at your decisions. Please ask yourself questions such as these…

- Does what I'm about to do line up with the Scriptures?
- What does God think about this?
- Will this help me grow?
- Will this affect my testimony?

The process you use to make a decision is extremely important, and, as you've heard me say, success and failure will always be just a few steps away from one another.

Jesus told us that the trail of a righteous man really is narrow at times. During His years on earth, the Lord restricted Himself to such a narrow way of living. In fact, He would only say what His Father was saying and do what His Father was doing. It sounds so restrictive, but it's actually a very freeing and releasing way to live. The narrow path of Jesus leads to the largest place of all.

I just wanted to remind you of a few things I've learned—and a few of the vistas I've enjoyed—along that narrow trail.

Foundations

You Can Trust Your Bible

Your words were found, and I ate them,

and Your word was to me the joy

and rejoicing of my heart;

for I am called by Your name,

O LORD God of hosts.

JEREMIAH 15:16

As you know, I believe the Bible to be God's written word, inerrant and infallible. I hope you will always make it your greatest treasure.

If I can't be there with you when times get hard and the walls close in (and they will), I want you to remember this most basic truth: You can trust your Bible.

You can! I have staked my life on it. I have staked my eternal salvation on it. Psalm 19:7 says this law of the Lord is perfect, or complete. It is capable of and adequate for meeting every need. It is complete in that it analyzes and addresses all sides of every issue you and I must face in our lives.

Do you remember Job's response, after he lost everything he had?

> I have not departed from the commandment
> of His lips; I have treasured the words of
> His mouth more than my necessary food.
> (Job 23:12)

What portion of God's Word do you think Job had access to? The Bible doesn't say, but it couldn't have been more than a fraction of what you and I are privileged to possess. Yet he clung to it with all his strength.

Here was a man who had been stripped of everything—land, cattle, income, health, and *all* his children, seven strong sons and three beautiful daughters. How did he even get up in the morning? How did he face the day? How did he survive? He went back to that which cannot change: the enduring Word of God. It became as necessary to his survival as food for the stomach.

In Psalm 19, David can't seem to say enough about the value of God's Word in a person's life. It converts the soul. It makes naive and undiscerning people wise. It brings joy to the heart. It gives insight to the eyes. It will never be dated or obsolete. It is completely righteous, true, and just. So when you are looking for wisdom, joy, and blessing, look to God's Word.

Do you remember the story of Ali Hafed? He was a wealthy, contented farmer who had wide fields, beautiful orchards, and lush gardens.

Then one day a man told him about diamonds.

The man told Ali how wealthy he *could* be if he owned a diamond mine. For the first time in many years, Ali Hafed went to bed that night discontented.

Diamonds! He craved such a mine. He hungered for such wealth. In his mind's eye, he could see the gems sparkle and flash with a thousand colors. He could see himself running his hands through piles of the glimmering stones. Why, it would be like possessing the very stars of heaven.

Soon Ali sold his farm and began a long search across the world for such a mine. He traveled many weary miles in strange and hostile places, finally becoming poor, broken, and defeated. In this depressed condition, on a gray morning far from home, Ali Hafed took his own life.

One day, the man who purchased Ali Hafed's farm led his camel into the garden to drink. As his camel put its nose into the shallow water of the garden brook, the farmer noticed a curious flash of light. He pulled out a rough black stone, which reflected all the hues of the rainbow.

A diamond! The man had discovered what would become the diamond mine of Golcanda, the most significant diamond mine in the history of the world. Had Ali Hafed remained at home and dug in his own fields, he would have had acres of diamonds. For every acre of that old farm—yes, every shovelful of soil—afterward revealed gems which since have decorated the crowns of monarchs.

I won't belabor the point. You can search the world over for wisdom and knowledge and secrets of success. You can travel and study for endless years in the greatest universities of the world. But you need go no further than the Bible at your bedside for the greatest treasury of wisdom in all the world. Scripture, of course, points us to the Lord Jesus, "in whom are hidden all the treasures of wisdom and knowledge" (Colossians 2:3).

We live in a world where people are scurrying everywhere, turning over every rock, trying everything to find fulfillment and happiness. But I just want you to remember that everything you need—everything pertaining to wisdom and love and success and happiness and life everlasting—lies between the covers of God's Word.

You don't have to search the world over for the deepest, richest mine. You already own it. It is your heritage and legacy.

The Spirit Will Be Your Teacher

"All this I have spoken while still with you.
But the Counselor, the Holy Spirit, whom the Father
will send in my name, will teach you all things
and will remind you of everything I have said to you."
JOHN 14:25–26, NIV

The Bible is the only book in the world where the Author comes to personally teach you the truths contained within. The Holy Spirit Himself will be your Teacher as you open up the pages of God's Word with a seeking, hungry heart.

There will come a time when you and I don't have the opportunity to sit together and talk about the Word and its implications for our lives. But when that day comes, there will be One who is always there, always with you, always eager to illuminate the text for you.

I can remember times in my life when I was about to make a decision that I knew in my heart was wrong. And as I was beginning to turn in that direction, the Holy Spirit would flash a Scripture across the screen of my mind. I could see the very words out of my own Bible. I could see the actual page and portion of the page where the verse was located.

The Spirit used what I knew of Scripture to warn me and direct me onto the right path. He uses what you know, Son. He uses what you are learning, what you are mining out of Scripture for yourself. Then, in those times when you're about to take an important step or make a critical decision, the Spirit will pull those verses out of your memory and allow them to come before your spiritual eyes. He'll keep you from doing things you might otherwise have done, had you not known the mind and heart of God.

Let me remind you of a few things I've learned from others that have helped me as I approach God's Word. As you open its pages, look for practical counsel, commands to be obeyed, facts to be known, examples to be followed, and promises to be enjoyed.

Here are a few guidelines Paul left for his young

friend in the ministry in 2 Timothy 3:16. "All Scripture," Paul wrote, "is given by inspiration of God." He goes on to explain how it is profitable in several areas of life.

- *It is profitable for doctrine: It shows us what to do.*
- *It is profitable for reproof: It shows us what not to do.*
- *It is profitable for correction: It shows us what to do when we didn't do what we were supposed to do!*
- *It is profitable for instruction in righteousness: It shows us how to stay on the track leading to blessing and fruitfulness.*

Son, if you believe your old dad, then please hold on to this bit of counsel: You will never, ever regret the time you have invested in the careful, prayerful study of God's Word. It will pay out a thousandfold dividend—today, tomorrow, and for as long as you live.

One "Formula"

That Won't Fail You

"Is not my word like fire," declares the LORD,
"and like a hammer that breaks a rock in pieces?"

JEREMIAH 23:29, NIV

I've never been big on formulas.

To me, most of them are about as valuable as yesterday's gum drying on the bedpost. Just glance at the titles of magazine articles as you go through the checkout line. Everyone has a formula to offer for just about anything.

The problem with formulas is that once we've learned one, we no longer feel the necessity to depend on the Lord in that area of life. We begin to function more out of habit than in relationship with Him. We develop grooves or patterns of living that never change because we never take time to ask the Lord if change might be necessary.

But having said all that…I do have one formula I'd like to offer.

This formula isn't seasonal; it's eternal. It's also simple. Here it is: *The Word is the basis upon which the Spirit acts.*

When someone tells you, "God is doing a new thing," then look to the Word. Long ago I learned that "if it's new, it's not the truth; and if it's the truth, it's not new."

Some people will say, "Listen to me! I've received a new revelation. God has shown me something new." But the truth is, God isn't saying anything new. He hasn't "learned" anything new lately. If God is speaking today, it is already in His Word and will be confirmed there.

Only a life built on God's Word and bathed in His Spirit will be effective. Any change that occurs in your life will be accomplished by the Word of God through the Spirit of God.

I can't impress upon you enough, Son, the need to read your Bible. I'm not talking as much about studying the Word as I am about letting the Word study *you.* Through the pages of Scripture, the Lord shines His searching, probing light into all the areas of your life. His Word walks through every room of your soul.

There are no closed doors to the Searcher of hearts.

The author of Hebrews wrote:

> For the word of God is living and powerful,
> and sharper than any two-edged sword,
> piercing even to the division of soul and
> spirit, and of joints and marrow, and is a
> discerner of the thoughts and intents of the
> heart. (Hebrews 4:12)

Let the Word of God analyze your life and show you where you need to change or grow. No, you don't need to fly through twenty chapters a day…just read the Book. When you sense the Spirit saying, "Pause and think about that," then obey Him. *Filling your mind with His mind should be a top priority in all of life.*

And one more thing. I've found that this exposure of our lives to God's truth has to be more than a once a week or a haphazard proposition. The book of Hebrews also says this:

> But exhort one another daily, while it is
> called "Today," lest any of you be hardened
> through the deceitfulness of sin.
> (Hebrews 3:13)

What a sobering thought. It may not take more than *a single day* to become hardened by Satan's deceits. But if we are walking in the refreshing rain of God's wisdom every day of our lives—be it morning, noon, or evening—our souls will be kept tender and responsive to His voice.

> Search me, O God, and know my heart;
> try me and know my anxious thoughts;
> and see if there be any hurtful way in me,
> and lead me in the everlasting way.
> (Psalm 139:23–24, NASB)

Keep God First

And God spoke all these words,
saying: "I am the LORD your God,
who brought you out of the land of Egypt,
out of the house of bondage.
You shall have no other gods before Me."

EXODUS 20:1-3

I'm often asked, "What's the hardest thing about being a pastor of a large church? What is the greatest burden you feel in the ministry: Preaching? Counseling? Administering?"

You need to know that my answer is "none of the above."

While any one of these tasks can be daunting or demanding on any given day, there is something even more difficult. As a matter of fact, I could be dazzling everyone every week with my sermons, saving marriages every day in counseling, and administering a

staff and budget the size of the Pentagon's, and still
be a miserable failure in my Lord's eyes.

The greatest challenge I face every day of my life
is probably the very one that you will face every day
too. It is keeping God first—maintaining a close, personal, growing relationship with Jesus Christ.

Our number one task as believers is to make sure
that nothing—no "god," person, object, task, duty, or
pleasure—comes before Him in our priorities, our
plans, or our affections.

This is no small thing! The good folks in the
church at Ephesus worked extremely hard, kept
their hopes alive, stayed doctrinally sound, and
patiently endured suffering for the Lord's name. Yet
the Lord Jesus said they were on the razor edge of
losing both their light and their witness in the world.
Why? Because "you have left your first love"
(Revelation 2:4).

Hard work and good teaching and a willingness
to stand in the gap for the Lord aren't enough. This
is a relationship, and the Lord is very, very concerned
with the condition of our hearts toward Him.

King Solomon would have known the first command from boyhood. And I would guess it was very
much on his mind when he wrote these words: "Trust

in the LORD with all your heart and lean not on your own understanding; in all your ways acknowledge him, and he will make your paths straight" (Proverbs 3:5–6, NIV).

"All of our ways" means all of our opportunities and undertakings. The word *acknowledge* doesn't mean to "know Him" just by studying about Him, but rather through a personal relationship with Him. *The Living Bible* paraphrases verse 6 like this: "In everything you do, put God first, and he will direct you and crown your efforts with success."

That's pretty much the bottom line, isn't it? In everything you do, Son, put God first, so He can direct your path. What does that mean? It means He not only gives you direction, but He commits Himself to removing any hindrances or obstacles that stand in the way of His destined purpose for you. He will make the path straight before you.

But notice that this statement is conditional. It tells you very specifically that you must not lean on or trust in your own understanding. Why? Because that understanding is inadequate, limited, and flawed by sin. The Bible says, "There is a way which seems right to a man, but its end is the way of death" (Proverbs 14:12).

✦ ✦ ✦

I was in New England once, speaking to a group of pastors at a retreat center out in a wilderness area. It was very cold, and we'd just experienced a major snowstorm. One beautiful, moonlit night, one of the pastors slipped out of bed, put on some snowshoes, and headed off into the woods for a walk. He went alone, with no flashlight or compass or provisions of any sort.

He never marked his trail, never looked at his watch, and paid no attention to landmarks. After a couple hours of wandering in the still, silver moonlight, he suddenly realized he was becoming very, very cold. And in that same instant he was jarred by another realization: "I'm lost! I have no idea how to get back!"

He certainly hadn't planned on getting lost. He just wasn't thinking. For some reason, he had a false sense of confidence that he could easily find his way back in the dark. But he couldn't. Others had to search for him in the night and the bitter cold, and they eventually found him…cold, embarrassed, but thankfully none the worse for his midnight wanderings.

That's the deceptiveness of the path that the world offers you. It looks good, it looks inviting, it seems fine, until it suddenly dawns on you: "I don't know where I am! I've wandered into something and have no idea how to go back or get out of this." You're lost in the woods at night. You're out in the cold, and it's too dark to follow your own tracks home.

Those without the guidance of God's Word and God's Spirit—for all of their sincerity or lofty motives or desire to be good people and good parents and good citizens—will walk into heartache after heartache, disaster after disaster. They can't help it! As Jesus said, "They are blind guides leading the blind, and both will fall into a ditch" (Matthew 15:14, TLB).

As I write these words, I'm thinking about the transitions in your life as a young man. For the next five to ten years, you're going to see a freight train of challenges and changes. College. Sports opportunities. Career options. Romance. Marriage. Establishing a home. The list goes on and on. And those are just the *expected* changes. You know as well as I do that it's those unexpected obstacles and those unforeseen twists and turns in the road that really take us to the limits of our understanding and ability to cope.

The best way to prepare for any transition in life, large or small, is to keep God first…to begin each day of our lives by yielding control of the steering wheel to Him.

When you think about it, why should I ever want to put anyone or anything in front of Him? Why should I tolerate other gods in my life? Why should I look for other saviors? Why should I serve lesser lords? He promised to provide for me everything I need. My life has completely changed, so why not tell the whole world what a mess I was when He found me? Jesus came along and took away my embarrassment and shame. Oh, how I love Him. That's the reason we can hold out hope for others. That's the reason we can say, "Put God first and He'll cover your past. If God has forgiven me, He can forgive you."

How could I not want to put such a God first?

It's not only the right thing to do, it's the wisest thing to do. He promises that if you look to Him first and keep Him first, you will find your life crowned with success.

Remember to Refresh

"Remember the Sabbath day, to keep it holy."

EXODUS 20:8

I'll never forget the day I woke up in the ICU to see a familiar face swim slowly into focus.

It was my dear friend Jack Hayford. As you know by now, Jack loves me very much. But even in my medicated state I knew that expression on his face. I had a hunch he hadn't flown up from Los Angeles to quote poetry to me. And I was right.

"Good enough for you?" he asked.

What kind of greeting was that for a friend in the ICU? What a strange thing to say to a man hanging on to life after a near-fatal heart attack. But Jack was just getting warmed up.

"You're a prideful man, Ron," he told me. "You think people are really impressed that you work seven days a week."

I groaned. As one of my closest friends for many years, Jack has certainly earned the right to speak to me that way. What's more, I knew that he was right. I had violated one of God's life principles, and I was paying the price.

You need to know I've always struggled with the fourth commandment. If I had been doing it—if they were Mehl's Ten Commandments—"Remember the Sabbath" probably would have ended up number 47. Or maybe 202. Sure, it's important. But alongside murder and adultery and coveting your neighbor's wife? Come on!

I've pastored the same church for twenty-five years. It's my life. I love the Lord's people. I love my responsibilities. I love being a shepherd. And through the years, for countless weeks at a time, I have been at the church seven days a week. Not five. Not six. Every day.

There are so many needs. So much hurt. So much opportunity. So many open doors. I keep wrestling with the idea that God "needs" more and more of me to get His work done.

But the truth is, Son, I need more and more of Him. As the church continues to grow, and the condition of families becomes more desperate, and the demands of the ministry go through the roof, I need more of His peace, more of His joy, more of His tenderness, more of His tough love, more of His wisdom, more of His resurrection life flowing through me.

I think you'll find that the same is true for you. And the simple fact is He isn't going to give what you need in one-minute bursts between sales appointments or on your coffee break.

He wants time with you.

He wants to walk with you.

He wants to share His heart with you.

He wants a relationship.

No matter where you are in the years ahead, you'll find that giving yourself over to workaholism or nonstop activities will be a great temptation. Overwork is celebrated by some and demanded by others. If you own your own company, you've made a great investment, so you feel the need to press the limits of physical and emotional strength to protect your investment.

But God has made a great investment in you, too. Give Him the chance to check on one of His most precious assets—you. Give it to Him often. He knows we desperately need such times. It's as though our spirits were equipped with a rechargeable battery, and we simply run down after a while. The current becomes very weak, the light in our hearts becomes very dim, and it affects every other part of our lives. Every relationship. Every project. Everything we touch. God knows our need to be restored, and during that time of rest, that's what happens.

My advice is to find a time and place where you enjoy meeting the Lord—just the two of you. Any spot will do. History tells us that the eleventh-century monk Brother Lawrence felt closest to the Lord while he was in the kitchen scrubbing pots and pans. He felt it was an interruption in his conversation with God when the bell rang for prayer time! God was so much a part of his kitchen duties that drying his hands and leaving for the chapel was just a bother. For you, that choice time with Him may be early in the morning, when the light of the new day sends little golden fingers into your room. Maybe it's during lunch hour, with half the day gone and half still to go. Maybe it's late at night after everyone has gone to bed.

Or maybe, if you're like me and you've neglected one of His commandments, it's time to *renew* those meeting times with the Lord—and you start that renewal from a hospital bed.

There's nothing wrong with that.

It's never too late to rekindle your relationship with God. It's always the right time to seek Him. He's ready when you are, where you are.

He just wants to be with you.

He Is Listening

I waited patiently for the LORD;

And He inclined to me,

And heard my cry.

PSALM 40:1

Every boy growing up probably gets invited at least once to go on a snipe hunt. If you accept, you're not likely to forget it!

According to *Webster's*, snipe are wading birds related to the woodcock, living chiefly in marshy places and characterized by a long, flexible bill used in digging.

You ever wonder why anyone would want to hunt a snipe? I suppose you could eat one—although I've never heard of anyone trying it. What I've always heard is that people are invited on snipe hunts for the sheer sporting thrill of it all…or something like that.

A friend of mine named Tim went on his first

(and last) snipe expedition at the tender age of nine. The invitation came from his two older brothers and an older cousin while the family was visiting his uncle's farm in eastern Nebraska. Tim appreciated being included, but couldn't quite figure why his normally aloof big brothers were suddenly so interested in doing something *with him*.

Tim's brothers and cousin informed him that they would embark on the hunt after sundown, and would stalk their quarry in the long, densely wooded shelterbelt at the east edge of the cornfield. His weapons for the hunt were a burlap gunnysack and a chunk of wood, for a club.

That evening, little Tim found himself crouching in the gloomy shadows of the shelterbelt, burlap bag open, wooden club at the ready. The older boys had headed off through the brush with clubs of their own. Their plan was to drive the elusive snipe out of hiding and—hopefully—into Tim's waiting gunnysack.

The boys were gone a long time. Little brother began feeling very alone in the darkness, under the whispering cottonwoods. He was getting tired of bending over with the sack. Worse yet, he was being eaten alive by a horde of hungry Nebraska mosquitoes.

Still more time went by and inky darkness descended. An owl hooted in the distance. Mosquitoes whined around Tim's ears and bit through his thin T-shirt. He suddenly felt very lonely. He suddenly felt very afraid. He suddenly wondered if he had been had.

"You guys?"

There was no reply to his tentative call.

"You guys?"

Still no reply. Tim started to cry.

"YOU GUYS?!"

"I'm here, son."

The reassuring voice of Tim's father suddenly cut through the night. And then his dad came striding out of the darkness, put his arm around him, and walked him back through the cornfield toward the welcoming lights of the distant farmhouse.

His brothers and cousin were already back at the house, of course, guffawing, stuffing their faces with Aunt Lucy's peach pie, and protesting mightily between bites that Dad had "ruined everything."

"Oh, those boys," Aunt Lucy clucked as she dabbed ointment on Tim's forty-seven mosquito bites.

As for the young snipe hunter, he was just glad to

be back in the refuge of the farmhouse, savoring his own dish of warm peach pie. And deep within him was the satisfaction that his dad had been "right there" the moment a note of desperation entered his voice. Tim's dad had somehow found out about the gag and determined beforehand that he wouldn't let it go too far.

That's a pretty good picture of a loving, tuned-in dad. It's also a good description of your heavenly Father. He is a Father who listens for your voice. You could be singing in the Billy Graham Crusade choir with ten thousand tongues, but He'd be listening for your voice, Son. You could kneel and pray with a multitude of intercessors, and yet He'd be listening for your petitions.

In Psalm 40, David found himself in a terrible situation. He wasn't on a snipe hunt, but really, it was even worse. He was in a pit. And not just any pit. This was "a horrible pit." This was a pit full of miry clay. This was a dark, slimy, smelly pit, and David was up to his neck in it. Later, after he was rescued, he wrote this account of his nightmare:

I waited patiently for the LORD;
And He inclined to me,

And heard my cry.
He also brought me up out of a horrible pit,
Out of the miry clay,
And set my feet upon a rock,
And established my steps.
He has put a new song in my mouth—
Praise to our God.
(Psalm 40:1–3)

Way down in that dark hole in the ground, David's cry must have sounded pretty faint, pretty weak. Someone walking by the top of the pit might not even have heard him.

But someone did hear. David's Father heard. And He did something about it.

David writes that the Lord "inclined to me, and heard my cry." In other words, God was "inclining" before David ever opened his mouth; He was bending over to listen before David could even muster the strength to cry out. And as soon as David spoke, the Lord came striding out of the darkness to lend a strong hand.

Did you know that the Lord listens for your voice? Has it entered your thinking today that the mighty Creator of galaxies and star systems and worlds beyond number gets down on one knee to look you in the eyes and focus on your needs? Think of it! God actually hears your faintest cry. He hears you when you are only thinking about calling for help. He hears you when you don't know any words to say at all, but can only groan deep within your spirit.

Even when it's night.

Even when you're lost.

Even when Satan leads you on a long snipe hunt in the dark and you're left holding an empty bag and you can't find your way home.

God strides out of the darkness and says, "I'm right here, son. I hear every word. Let's go have a piece of pie."

Character

Wisdom Unmasks Life

For the LORD gives wisdom;
From His mouth come knowledge and understanding.

PROVERBS 2:6

In school, you learn that your whole future is based on education and knowledge. If you lack degrees, you're told, you lack a future.

I'm not disagreeing with that. I just want to make sure you remember that while man values intelligence and knowledge, God prizes *wisdom*.

Why is wisdom so essential? Because God's wisdom gives us one of the choicest gifts you and I could ever attain...*perspective*. Can you and I—earthbound, timebound, shortsighted creatures that we are—even begin to understand how essential and valuable perspective is?

God, who dwells in heaven (above the earth) and eternity (beyond the constraints of time), offers us a view of life we could never obtain any other way.

The book of Proverbs, for example, shows us the consequences that come into the life of an unwise person—and what happens to people who become "wise in their own eyes."

Wisdom produces prudence, which means "to make bare." It lets you strip off the mask, and gets you down to the unadorned facts of a circumstance or situation. You will be able to see behind the scenes…you will be able to see through the glitter and shallow exteriors, and you will know better what you're really dealing with.

If I can't be around, then I must say that one of my greatest desires is that you will tap into God's wisdom and become a truly wise person.

Because if you are wise, you'll be able to unmask things that others can't. You'll be able to see beneath things that aren't what they appear to be. You'll have a perspective on life that can only come from knowing the treasures of the wisdom of God Himself.

Proverbs teaches us about God's ways and how to apply them to our lives. Real wisdom is seeing life the way it truly is. You know which choice to make. You know which road to take. And you know something of the consequences of the choice you're making before you make it.

There are times when I've had to ask myself,
"Now, why did he do that? Why did she do that?
Why did he steal that car? Why did she leave her
husband and kids? Why did that boy shoplift? Why
did that woman sell her soul to get ahead in business?
Why did that bright young teen become sexually
active?"

The answer is, because they are *simple*. They are
unwise, lacking in common sense and insight. They
are open to everything in the world except wise counsel.

What happens to an unwise person? What happens to those who ignore godly wisdom? The book of
Proverbs leaves no doubt. Please take time to ponder
these verses.

■ **They follow the counsel of fools...and must endure
the same penalty.**

My son, if sinners entice you, do not give in
to them. If they say, "Come along with us;
let's lie in wait for someone's blood, let's
waylay some harmless soul; let's swallow
them alive...we will get all sorts of valuable
things and fill our houses with plunder;

throw in your lot with us, and we will share
a common purse"—my son, do not go
along with them…. These men lie in wait
for their own blood; they waylay only
themselves! Such is the end of all who go
after ill-gotten gain; it takes away the lives
of those who get it.
(Proverbs 1:10–12, 13–15, 18–19, NIV)

■ **They convince themselves there will be no
consequences to their actions.**

The woman Folly is loud; she is undisci-
plined and without knowledge. She sits at
the door of her house, on a seat at the high-
est point of the city, calling out to those who
pass by, who go straight on their way. "Let
all who are simple come in here!" she says
to those who lack judgment. "Stolen water
is sweet; food eaten in secret is delicious!"
But little do they know that the dead are
there, that her guests are in the depths of
the grave. (Proverbs 9:13–18, NIV)

■ **They lose all powers of discernment.**

A simple man believes anything, but a prudent man gives thought to his steps.
(Proverbs 14:15, NIV)

When Solomon, the writer of these proverbs, was facing the most demanding and challenging hour of his life, God said, in effect, "Solomon, what do you need? What do you want? Whatever you ask, I'll give it to you."

The young king didn't ask for money, power, influence, or the life of his enemies. Instead he said, "Lord, I just need wisdom. I'm overwhelmed by the responsibilities before me. I need great discernment to lead Your people" (See 1 Kings 3).

Pleased with that request, God granted Solomon not only what he'd asked for, but also many of the things he hadn't asked for.

How did a young man like Solomon know to ask for wisdom? I believe it was because of what he learned from his father, David. He learned to value wisdom beyond anything else in life, so that when the crisis moment came and God said, "Son, ask of Me whatever you will," he knew the very words to say.

It's the prayer of my life that, in those crisis moments when life is on the line, you, too, will remember to ask the Lord God for wisdom and discernment.

The wisdom of God is found in His Word and fleshed out in our lives. In Proverbs 1, wisdom speaks.

> Wisdom calls aloud in the street, she raises
> her voice in the public squares; at the head
> of the noisy streets she cries out, in the gate-
> ways of the city she makes her speech:
> "How long will you simple ones love your
> simple ways? How long will mockers
> delight in mockery and fools hate knowl-
> edge? If you had responded to my rebuke, I
> would have poured out my heart to you and
> made my thoughts known to you. But since
> you rejected me when I called and no one
> gave heed when I stretched out my hand,
> since you ignored all my advice and would
> not accept my rebuke, I in turn will laugh at

your disaster; I will mock when calamity
overtakes you....

"For the waywardness of the simple will
kill them, and the complacency of fools will
destroy them; but whoever listens to me will
live in safety and be at ease, without fear of
harm." (Proverbs 1:20–26, 32–33, NIV)

The Bible says that a person can willfully reject
the wisdom of God. But when you do, life becomes
difficult, unmanageable, and very, very dangerous.
You must endure the heartbreak of constant frustration and in the end...self-destruction.

Notice that Wisdom, here personified as a great
and gracious lady, is *in the streets*. What does that
mean? Someone once explained it to me like this: It
isn't as though Wisdom is standing on a street corner
with a big sandwich board declaring, "You've found
me! I am Wisdom!"

What, then, does it mean? *It means you will learn
from experience.* Others will make bad decisions and
meet with disaster. Others will reject God's counsel,
stiffen their necks, and go their own way, and you
will learn when they weep over their failures. You
will learn when they destroy themselves and others.

You will learn from their mistakes—and from your own as well.

That, I believe, is "wisdom in the streets."

The wisdom of God cries out to a naive world and says, "When will you learn that the world's way leads to trouble, hardship, and disappointment? When will you open your eyes and see what happens to those who reject My ways and My offer of salvation?"

How, then, do you obtain such wisdom? It really isn't difficult at all. *Just ask*, the Bible says.

> If any of you lacks wisdom, he should ask
> God, who gives generously to all without
> finding fault, and it will be given to him.
> (James 1:5, NIV)

Isn't that amazing? If you desire the greatest treasure in the entire world, you obtain it simply by asking for it. From the context of this passage in James, I believe the Bible teaches that wisdom is especially available to us in times of tests and trials and challenges. James begins the chapter talking about what to do when all kinds of trials enter your life. It is a time of testing and pressure. *But the wisdom of God was made for such a time as this and is freely available to you.*

Do you see the importance of this context? We don't ask God for wisdom because we want to be some all-wise, white-bearded sage sitting on a mountaintop with all the answers. No, the whole reason for tapping into God's great wisdom is for those times when we are confused, fearful, perplexed, or in pain. It is in those times that we cry out for discernment and find God more than willing to give us the direction and help we need.

Why should you seek wisdom? So that you can handle situations as they come up in your life, and so that you can interpret times and circumstances from God's eternal perspective. Wisdom, above all, is skill at living. It's the ability to navigate your way through life.

Solomon says:

If you call out for insight and cry aloud for understanding, and if you look for it as for silver and search for it as for hidden treasure, then you will understand the fear of the LORD and find the knowledge of God. For the LORD gives wisdom, and from his mouth come knowledge and understanding. (Proverbs 2:3–6, NIV)

What an astonishing offer. I suppose the question it really comes down to is this: How much do you want wisdom? How desperately do you desire it? The Bible assures us that if you truly seek it—and look for it in the right places—you will find it.

My prayer for you today—and until the day I go home to be with the Lord—is that you will desire His wisdom with all of your heart.

Forty Wrestlers

My heart is fixed, O God, my heart is fixed:

I will sing and give praise

PSALM 57:7, KJV

Let me tell you a great commitment story out of the Roman era. It may be a story you find yourself telling your own children someday.

The emperor Nero gathered around him some of the strongest, bravest, most athletic men of the empire and named them his own personal wrestlers: the Emperor's Wrestlers.

This was the "dream team" of the empire. They stood sentry around the Roman amphitheater and attended to the emperor at all times.

There was a famous statement — a motto — which, according to historians, they quoted often: "We, the wrestlers, wrestling for thee, O emperor, to win for thee the victory, and from thee the victor's crown."

On one occasion, the Roman army, including
these great wrestlers, was sent to Gaul to put down
some kind of rebellion. No soldiers were braver or
more capable than the Emperor's Wrestlers. A centurion by the name of Vespasian led them.

While they were in Gaul, historians tell us that
many of these wrestlers were converted to Jesus
Christ. Word came back to Nero that some of his personal wrestlers had become Christians. Immediately,
the emperor sent a message to Vespasian: "If there be
any among your soldiers who cling to the faith of the
Christians, they must die."

Vespasian received the decree in the dead of win-
ter in Gaul. The soldiers were encamped on the shore
of an inland lake. With a sinking heart, Vespasian read
the message. He called the soldiers together and asked,
"Have any of you embraced the Christian faith?"

Vespasian must have winced as forty of these
magnificent warriors stepped forward and saluted
him. He said, "I will give you until sundown tomorrow to deny this…or you must die."

At sundown the next day, he asked the same
question and the same forty stepped forward. He
said, "I cannot allow you to die at the hands of your

fellow soldiers. I will strip you naked and banish you to the middle of the lake, and must leave you to the elements."

So he had them stripped and sent them to the middle of the frozen lake in the dead of a freezing night. Not long after, he heard voices from across the ice: "Forty wrestlers, wrestling for Thee, O Christ, to win for Thee the victory, and from Thee the victor's crown." He heard it again and again through the night, the chant growing fainter and fainter as the morning came.

Finally, near dawn, one lonely figure staggered up to the fire. The man could stand the cold no longer. He came to warm himself, admitting he had denied Christ. And then came the cry faintly across the ice, "Thirty-nine wrestlers, wrestling for Thee, O Christ, to win for Thee the victory, and from Thee the victor's crown."

In that moment, God did something in Vespasian's heart. The centurion suddenly threw his helmet to the ground, stripped off his armor, and raced off across the ice, shouting at the top of his voice, "Forty wrestlers, wrestling for Thee, O Christ, to win for Thee the victory, and from Thee the victor's crown."

✦ ✦ ✦

God calls us to a life of commitment. He works in the midst of commitment and obedience. Satan, on the other hand, works best in the midst of passivity. If Satan can get you to do nothing, if he can get you to commit to nothing, he can neutralize your life. *Satan's greatest work is done when he convinces us that nothing needs to be done.*

If we listen to him, we'll begin to say things like this: "I'll do this tomorrow…. I'll do it next week…. It's not that important…. It's really no big deal…. No one will miss me if I'm not there…."

If you are passive in any area of your Christian life, Satan will eat you alive.

Some people believe that great blessing and victory in the Christian life "just happens." They say, "Oh, you're just so fortunate to have the kind of impact you have and to live the kind of life you do." But the truth is, success in the Christian life means commitment…a commitment to the Word, a commitment to prayer, a commitment to get alone with the Lord every day, a commitment to gain encouragement from fellow believers.

When I think back to my eighth-grade championship basketball team, I always remember the kid who was, without a doubt, the worst player on the squad. He had so few skills, I'm really not even sure how he made the team.

Yet at the end of the year, he was named Most Valuable Player.

The reason was this: No one was more committed. No one worked harder in practice. No one had a better attendance record. No one was more encouraging to other members of the team. And at the end of the year, the guys couldn't think of anyone who had been more valuable to our team.

God is looking for more than giftedness; He's looking for people who will commit to His calling and His will.

All commitment, however, will be tested! If you say you want to live an uncompromised life, you will find that determination tried by fire. Paul was uncompromising, and who was tested more than he? At one point in his life, he wrote about his experience:

- I have worked harder than any of them.
- I have served more prison sentences!
- I have been beaten times without number.
- I have faced death again and again.

- I have been beaten the regulation thirty-nine stripes by the Jews five times.
- I have been beaten with rods three times.
- I have been stoned once.
- I have been shipwrecked three times.
- I have been twenty-four hours in the open sea.

In my travels I have been in constant danger from rivers, from bandits, from my own countrymen, and from pagans. I have faced danger in city streets, danger in the desert, danger on the high seas, danger among false Christians. I have known drudgery, exhaustion, many sleepless nights, hunger and thirst, fasting, cold and exposure. Apart from all external trials I have the daily burden of responsibility for all the churches.
(2 Corinthians 11:26–29, *Phillips*)

Talk about testing someone's commitment! That doesn't sound like a life, it sounds like a walking nightmare. And yet listen to Paul's conclusion:

But none of these things move me; nor do I
count my life dear to myself, so that I may
finish my race with joy, and the ministry
which I received from the Lord Jesus, to
testify to the gospel of the grace of God.
(Acts 20:24)

None of those things moved him? Come on,
Paul! How could that be?

Here was the apostle's secret: The goal before
him was so captivating, so radiant, so desirable, that
he could keep on running right through the pain and
frustration and danger. He was committed to reach-
ing his goal! Listen to his voice once again:

Not that I have already obtained all this, or
have already been made perfect, but I press
on to take hold of that for which Christ
Jesus took hold of me. Brothers, I do not
consider myself yet to have taken hold of it.
But one thing I do: Forgetting what is
behind and straining toward what is ahead,
I press on toward the goal to win the prize
for which God has called me heavenward in
Christ Jesus. (Philippians 3:12–14, NIV)

✦ ✦ ✦

I've heard it said somewhere that discipline is giving up your today for God's tomorrow. I need to make decisions in my life today—even if they mean some discomfort and strain and self-denial—that I know will bring honor and glory to the Lord tomorrow.

Integrity

Because I love your commands more than gold,

more than pure gold, and because I consider

all your precepts right, I hate every wrong path.

PSALM 119:127–128, NIV

Sometimes it's hard to sell people on the value of integrity. From all outward appearances, it doesn't "pay" to be honest.

There were certainly times in the life of Joseph when he must have been tempted to say, "What *good* has it done to me to walk the straight path?" (See Genesis 39–41.) Here was a young man who remained committed to integrity no matter what the cost. Sold into slavery by his own brothers, he was eventually falsely accused and thrown into a dungeon before finally being vindicated by the Lord.

Joseph could certainly have prayed the prayer of David, uttered centuries later: "You have preserved my life because I am innocent; you have brought me

into your presence forever" (Psalm 41:12, NLT).
Joseph lived his life in God's presence, with the
knowledge of God's watchful eye.

Here's a bit of truth I want you to hold onto, Son.
When Joseph ran from the crude seduction of
Potiphar's wife, he wasn't just running from a
woman. *He was running from anything that would abort
God's purposes in his life.*

Do you remember what he told that adulteress
(probably again and again)?

"How then could I do such a wicked thing
and sin against God?" (Genesis 39:9, NIV)

He chose God's way. He chose to see God's purpose fulfilled in his life rather than fulfilling a passing
fleshly fancy. He *feared* losing the sense of God's presence and the touch of God's blessing upon his life.
That's why he didn't walk or stroll away from that
woman; he RAN. God-given discretion preserved his
life (Proverbs 2:11).

Son, you know how I have earnestly desired
God's blessing on my ministry in our church through
the years. You know how I have feared doing anything or saying anything that might jeopardize that

blessing. What a terrible thing it would be to lose the hand of God's favor on my family, the church, or my life because of some foolish, ill-considered action or decision. I pray such a thing will never happen to me...or to you.

Integrity says that what I am in public, I also am in private. Integrity is what you do when you're alone, with no one's eye upon you but the Lord's. Satan, the adversary, is looking for a foothold in every one of our lives. He's looking for those places where our public lives do not match our private lives—leaving an integrity gap. It is in such "gaps" that he finds a handhold or a toehold, gaining access to our lives. Like a skilled climber, Satan doesn't need much of a foothold to advance. Anything that isn't surrendered or submitted to God becomes a hand-hold or foothold for the enemy.

If you choose to live a life of integrity like Joseph, everything in your life must be filtered through the grid of God's approval. (Growth in holiness means that "grid" becomes finer and finer through the years, gradually filtering out things we once participated in and approved of.)

That filter works another way, too. You will realize that nothing touches your life apart from God's knowledge and approval. Everything that comes into your experience is filtered through God's fingers of love. What a wonderful assurance! And I know that if God allows something to touch my life, He will also give me the grace and strength to deal with it.

It is a fact, Son, that the most crucial decisions of your life will be made when you are all alone. Decisions of integrity are made by young people who find themselves alone in a room and choose to turn off the TV when a questionable movie or program comes on. They're made by people who won't compromise their beliefs or personal standards to "get ahead."

The most significant choices you make in life won't be made in the middle of a crowd, with lots of people standing around. They will be made in the private times when only God sees what you are doing.

When you live a life of integrity, you will know the favor of God. When Joseph was in slavery, Scripture tells us, "The LORD was with Joseph and blessed him greatly as he served in the home of his Egyptian master" (Genesis 39:2, NLT). When Joseph was falsely accused and imprisoned in the Pharaoh's dungeon, we read: "But the LORD was with Joseph there, too, and he granted Joseph favor with the chief jailer" (Genesis 39:21, NLT).

God was with Joseph when he was prosperous, sailing along with favorable winds on a calm sea. But God was also with Joseph in the storm—in the midst of great trouble, turmoil, and trial. In either situation, when God is with you, you never have to worry. If you're a person of integrity, it doesn't matter where you are or what the circumstances of your life might be. You can have the inner confidence that the Lord is with you, and will see you through.

This is what I want for my sons, for my grand-children, and for you.

> *Lord, make us choose the harder right,*
> *rather than the easier wrong.*
> *And to never be contented with half-truths,*
> *when whole truths can be won.*
> *Endow us with courage that is born of*
> *loyalty to all that is noble and worthy,*
> *that scorns to compromise with vice and injustice,*
> *and knows no fear when right and*
> *truth are in jeopardy. Amen.*

THE CADET'S PRAYER.
WEST POINT MILITARY ACADEMY

The Path of Favor and Joy

"If you do what is right, will you not be accepted?

But if you do not do what is right,

sin is crouching at your door;

it desires to have you, but you must master it."

GENESIS 4:7, NIV

Let me make you a promise, Son.

If you obey God in every situation, He'll handle the outcomes in your life. You won't even have to worry about them, because the outcomes in your life will be His responsibility, not yours.

But if you consistently disobey the Lord and His Word, then He no longer makes Himself responsible. You become responsible for the outcomes in your life.

That's why we see so many people in the world who manipulate and scheme and cheat and backstab and crawl right over people to get what they want. Why do they do it? Because they're on their own! They truly do have to "look out for number one" because they have chosen their own path, rather than the Lord's.

I've learned that when you obey God, He'll fight for you; He'll be in your corner. But I've also learned (the hard way) that if you disobey Him, then you'll find Him fighting against you, challenging you at every turn. It's called resisting the proud. It's God's way of working to bring us back to reality, where we'll trust Him for everything.

As a pastor, I hear people saying things like this: "The devil is after me. Satan has hindered me and tripped me up." I don't doubt that's true at times. But I also want you to know that when an individual is living in disobedience to known truth, God Himself will allow challenges into that life to turn him or her to Himself and back to the path of obedience.

It wasn't Satan who prepared a great fish to swallow Jonah, the disobedient prophet. It was the Lord. Jonah had thought he could disobey God and get away with it. When God sent Jonah on a mission trip to Nineveh, the prophet flatly refused. He got into a cargo ship and sailed in the opposite direction, toward Tarshish.

The prophet should have known better (and maybe he did). If you step out on God, He'll come after you. What's always fascinated me in this biblical account is that everyone and everything in the story is obedient…except Jonah, the Lord's own prophet.

The storm was obedient. So were the sailors on the ship. Ditto the great fish. So was a vine that grew up at God's command, and even the lowly worm that came along to chew on that vine. The wicked Ninevites themselves were obedient and greatly humbled themselves before the Lord after they heard His message of approaching judgment.

Jonah, however, ran the other way.

But God knows how to deal with His disobedient children. As the book of Hebrews states,

"My son, do not make light of the Lord's discipline, and do not lose heart when he rebukes you, because the Lord disciplines those he loves, and he punishes everyone he accepts as a son." Endure hardship as disci-

pline; God is treating you as sons. For what
son is not disciplined by his father?
(Hebrews 12:5–7, NIV)

God put a storm in the path of the prophet's disobedience and, as we all know, Jonah ended up
being the chosen vessel of God to bring a great and
mighty city to its knees in repentance. In the end he
obeyed, but what a long, unpleasant detour he had to
endure to get back on the path.

As your dad, I pray that you won't have to take
the long, hard route through life, when the path of
obedience would bring you such favor and joy in the
company of your family and of the Lord who loves
you.

Obedience

*"Has the LORD as great delight in burnt offerings
and sacrifices, as in obeying the voice of the LORD?
Behold, to obey is better than sacrifice,
and to heed than the fat of rams."*

1 SAMUEL 15:22

It's my belief, Son, that by your obedience you yourself will determine what God can do for you.

Let me explain. Scripture says, "Delight yourself also in the LORD, and He shall give you the desires of your heart" (Psalm 37:4). And if in fact you put Him first in your life, make Him Lord of your life, respond to His Word, and obey His voice, *you will actually be determining what He can do for you.*

Imagine a set of twins. Let's say they're seventeen and both going out on dates on a particular Friday night. Their dad has told them, "I want you both in by midnight, understood?" One of the twins obeys and gets home at a quarter to twelve. He says good night to his dad and mom and heads upstairs to bed.

The other twin doesn't make it in until a quarter to three. The door is locked, and he has to knock to get in. The father opens the door and says, "I told you twelve o'clock. It's two forty-five. We'll have to deal with this in the morning. Good night." And the second twin slinks up to his room and goes to bed.

Now...what do you think the results of that evening will be?

The twin who came in at eleven forty-five will probably be allowed to stay out until twelve-thirty the next week. But the twin who came in at two forty-five? Well, he won't be going out at all — probably for weeks to come. Oh, he will be forgiven. He will experience his parents' grace and love. But he will still have to endure the consequences of his disobedience.

Why? Because his parents are mean and restrictive? Not at all. He was the one who determined what they could and would do for him. His own actions, his own disobedience determined his future opportunities.

Son, it's been the joy of my heart to care for you and bless you. But as the years go by, I know I can't always be there for you. And when it comes to your relationship with the Lord God, who loves you more than I could ever love you, you will be the one who determines what He can do for you and how He can pour His favor into your life. And you will determine those things by your obedience to Him and your response to His Lordship.

Son, you won't remember this, but an incident comes to my mind from when you were just a little guy, four years old at the most.

I came into the house one afternoon and there you were, sitting on the floor, leaning up against a wall. I walked by and said, "Hi, Son, how are you?" and you didn't respond.

You didn't look up.

You didn't acknowledge me at all.

I got halfway down the hall and it dawned on me that you hadn't said anything. As I turned to head into my bedroom, the Lord seemed to speak to me.

Do you know what you've just taught your son?

"No, Lord, what?"

You've just taught him that doing your will is optional. He can answer you when he feels like answering; he can reply to you when he feels like replying. Is that what you want him to learn?

At the time, it hadn't seemed like such a big deal to me. But the Lord began to teach me that day that holding you accountable to respond to my voice would one day help you remember to respond to His voice, to His authority.

As I stood there in the hallway, the Lord gave me a sudden visual picture. And it was frightening. It was a picture of a sixteen-year-old adolescent, cursing me to my face after I'd asked him to do something.

So I immediately walked back down the hall into the living room. I knelt down, put my hands on your little shoulders, and looked you in the eye. You didn't like it; you knew you were being challenged, and you tried to squirm out of my grasp. But I held you firmly and said to you, "Son, when I speak to you, when I ask how you're doing, I really want to know." I learned that day that I needed to make sure I was sincere every time I asked you how you were doing.

The whole point of that encounter, I realized, was this: If I could speak to you and you felt you didn't have to respond, there would come a day when the Lord would speak to you, and you might think there were optional times to respond to Him, too.

If you had grown up with a father who was so busy and preoccupied that he didn't really mean it when he said, "How are you?" then you might have developed the idea that God didn't really mean it or didn't really care when He spoke to you.

But He does care about His walk and conversation with you. He is not preoccupied, and there is a sense of purpose and destiny in everything He says to you. I wanted you to understand some of those things at an early age, Son. I've always been thankful and grateful for your respect and obedience. But when I'm no longer around, I want you to remember to show the utmost respect and obedience to our Lord.

When He speaks to you, He means every word He says.

Everything God does on earth has its genesis in the obedience of His children. Everything of blessing and victory begins with obedience. *Scripture shows us again and again that simple acts of obedience are followed by mighty acts of God.*

You can build an ark, but only God can make it rain.

You can offer your little lunch of loaves and fish, but only God can multiply them to feed a multitude.

You can fight the Amorites to the best of your ability and the limits of your strength, but only God can make the sun stand still until that victory is complete.

As Joshua was about to lead Israel across the Jordan and into the Promised Land, the Lord gave him these words: "Study this Book of the Law continually. Meditate on it day and night so you may be sure to obey all that is written in it. Only then will you succeed" (Joshua 1:8, NLT).

That wouldn't have been "new information" for General Joshua. Just before his mentor, Moses, passed away, Joshua and the whole nation with him experienced a mighty object lesson. Representatives of six tribes stood on Mount Gerizim to shout forth all the blessings God would bring into the nation's life if the people followed the Lord and kept His law. Then, across the valley on Mount Ebal, representatives from six other tribes pronounced the curses that would fall on the people if they ceased following the Lord and obeying His decrees.

Obedience, then and now, is the pathway to all blessing and success.

Humility

He guides the humble in what is right

and teaches them his way.

PSALM 25:9, NIV

"Humility," said A. W. Tozer, "is as scarce as an albino robin." In other words, there may be a few flying around in this old world, but they are very, very rare.

That may be so, but oh, how our God *delights* in the humility of His redeemed sons and daughters!

Not long ago, I was invited to speak in front of fifteen thousand people at Bill and Gloria Gaither's annual "Praise Gathering" in Indianapolis, Indiana. I have to tell you, Son, I felt like a man sitting on top of the world.

After the service I found myself in the foyer, surrounded by the Gaithers and many other internationally known musicians and recording artists. Out of the corner of my eye, I noticed a little girl making her way through the group, holding her Bible open to

one of the blank pages as she collected the auto-
graphs of her favorite musicians and vocalists.

I felt humbled when she approached me.
Imagine...all those renowned people to be
admired...and this child was approaching me, a
preacher boy from Beaverton, Oregon.

She opened her Bible, handed it to me, and asked
if I would sign it. On the page she'd asked me to sign,
I noticed the signatures of some very gifted and
beloved people. As I took out my pen to write, she
looked up at me with wide eyes and asked breath-
lessly, "Are you one of the Gaither singers? Do you
make CDs? Are you *famous*?"

I smiled. "Well, no," I said. "I'm really not."

With that, she grabbed her Bible out of my hands,
closed it, and walked away without a word, leaving
me standing there with pen in hand. She didn't want
to be bothered with the rabble of common humanity,
she wanted the signatures of *somebodies*.

Boy, that got my feet back on the ground in a
hurry...right where they needed to be all along.

James chapter 4 says:

"God opposes the proud but gives grace to
the humble." Submit yourselves, then, to

God. Resist the devil, and he will flee from
you. Come near to God and he will come
near to you…. Humble yourselves before the
Lord, and he will lift you up.
(vv. 6–8, 10, NIV)

Humility, I have learned through the years, is a
choice.

It's not something done to you, but rather by you.
While I believe it's our job to humble ourselves, I also
know that God may challenge a proud individual
with a task that will exhaust his or her talents, skills,
and strength. He knows that we need to experience
the life and joy and provision we will find at the end
of ourselves.

I heard about a young Scottish preacher who
was very proud and self-centered. Invited to speak
before a great crowd of people, he started up the
steps to the platform with shoulders back and chest
out. He was feeling supremely confident and looking
very fine and proud.

As the young Scotsman stood up to speak, however, he lost his concentration. The thoughts wouldn't
flow. He stammered and stuttered but could not
recover his composure. After five or ten minutes of

utter embarrassment, he decided to cut his losses. He closed his Bible and walked dejectedly down the steps, shoulders slumped, and head bowed in humiliation.

As he walked quickly down the aisle, a dear elderly Scottish woman grabbed his coattail as he went by. "Laddie," she told him, "if you had gone oop the way you come doon, you might have come doon the way you had gone oop."

If anyone in the world experienced humbling, it was the apostle Peter. Here are a few hard-won insights from his journal....

■ **Humility is seeing God for who He is.**

Humble yourselves, therefore, under God's mighty hand, that he may lift you up in due time. Cast all your anxiety on him because he cares for you. (1 Peter 5:6–7, NIV)

In other words, humility does not consist of focusing on what I am not. It isn't a matter of saying, "Poor me. I'm nothing. I'm nobody. I guess I'll go eat some worms." It is rather focusing on the might and greatness of God.

■ **Humility is seeing yourself for who you are.**

Once you have seen God, you can (finally) see
yourself. Humility is seeing the real you...and
accepting it. It's not viewing yourself as worthless or
hopeless, but rather as one who is utterly dependent
upon Him. It's coming under His mighty hand. If you
rely on yourself, you won't rely on Him.

■ **Humility is seeing others for who they are.**

> Don't be selfish; don't live to make a good
> impression on others. Be humble, thinking
> of others as better than yourself. Don't
> think only about your own affairs, but be
> interested in others, too, and what they are
> doing. (Philippians 2:3–4, NLT)

Humility is realizing the value of those around
me, and placing greater value on them than on
myself. It's just a simple fact, Son: If you're too
impressed with you, you won't be impressed with
others.

I'm sure you've heard me say this many times before, but please hear me once again: If what God has called you to isn't bigger than you, it's probably not God's will.

To me, this is fundamental. If you don't come to the place of utter humiliation…if you don't come to the place of brokenness and weeping before the Lord…if you don't come to the realization that it is impossible for you to do what God has asked you to do and be what He has asked you to be—whether it's a son, a daughter, a husband, a wife, or a business-man—then you have yet to be humbled.

God wouldn't invite you to do something you could already accomplish, because then you wouldn't need Him! You wouldn't turn to Him or rely on Him. Humility is recognizing my dependence upon God for everything.

When parents bring their child before the church to be dedicated, what are they saying? They're say-ing, "We can't do this. We can do what we know to do, but what really needs to be done in this child's life only God can do."

I believe that very theme runs straight through all of our Christian experience.

Living Faith

What Is Faith?

Now faith means we have full confidence
in the things we hope for,
it means being certain of the things we cannot see.

HEBREWS 11:1, *PHILLIPS*

When it comes to faith in God, the odds are always irrelevant.

I love the story of how Gideon built up an army of Israelites to take on a host of Midianite invaders. The Lord said to him, "You have too many men for me to deliver Midian into their hands" (Judges 7:2, NIV).

Too many men? Did I hear You right, Lord?

Yes, he'd heard correctly. God didn't want anything approaching even odds for this encounter.

So prior to his very first military encounter, Gideon was obliged to send almost all of his soldiers home, leaving him a paltry three hundred men against a vast and powerful army. With that number, however, the Lord easily routed the enemy.

It doesn't matter what you face, Son. God is more than adequate.

In the movie *The Bear*, a little orphaned bear cub sticks close by a monster-sized grizzly, watching and imitating everything he does. One thing the cub observes is that when the great bear is confronted by a challenge, he rears up on his hind legs and let loose a great roar.

As the story progresses, the cub finds himself stalked by a cougar. The little guy is trembling, frightened half to death. But then he remembers what his big pal did in the presence of a challenger. Rearing up on his stubby little hind legs, he waves his paws in the air and roars as loudly as he can.

To the cub's surprise and delight, the big cat suddenly freezes in its tracks, turns tail, and runs like a shot into the woods. At this point the camera pans around and we can see that behind the little cub, the massive grizzly bear is standing on his hind legs, waving his huge paws and roaring.

When I first saw that scene, I had a mental picture of the Lord Jesus standing behind me. The truth is, Satan isn't much impressed with my puny roaring, with my threats, or with my determination. But he is very impressed with Jesus Christ. And with the mighty Son of God standing behind me, the enemy turns tail and flees.

Stepping Out in Doubt

And when Peter had come down out of the boat,

he walked on the water to go to Jesus.

But when he saw that the wind was boisterous,

he was afraid; and beginning to sink he cried out, saying,

"Lord, save me!" And immediately Jesus stretched out His

hand and caught him, and said to him,

"O you of little faith, why did you doubt?"

MATTHEW 14:29–31

Remember that wild, stormy night on the Sea of Galilee? Most people read the words of Jesus— "Why did you doubt?"—and take them as a sharp rebuke, as though Jesus were shaking a stern finger in Peter's face.

I don't see it that way. I think the Lord is saying, "I'm coming alongside you because I want to encourage your faith. You were doing so well! Why did you turn back?"

That, I believe, is what the Lord will do through all the days and moments of your life. In every situation He will constantly encourage you to grow, increase in faith, and trust Him more and more. Like a patient, loving Parent, He will help you advance from crawling to baby steps…from baby steps to walking…and from walking to running with strength and confidence.

In the lives of His disciples, virtually everything the Lord led them to experience in their three-year journey with Him was for one purpose: to develop their capacity for faith. Far from being the worst doubter on that turbulent night, Peter was leading the way in his faith. Who else climbed out of the boat that night? Who else fixed his eyes on Jesus, squared his shoulders, and started to hike across the waves? Not John. Not James. Not Philip. Not Andrew. It was Peter who threw natural caution into that wild wind and attempted the impossible.

"Lord," he shouted into the gale, "if it's really You, call me over to Your side."

Jesus said, "Come."

And Peter went.

Not far, maybe, but my goodness, give the man a little credit. He did walk on water! In those brief, miracle moments, the big fisherman came close—so very close—to entering a whole new phase of life, a whole new phase of belief. He was almost there!

Peter learned that night that he really did have faith enough to attempt mighty things. But he also learned how much further he had to go. He was growing, yes, but he hadn't arrived yet. His faith was still "little."

I believe that's the reason the Lord allows you and me to come up against those faith-stretching tests and those dead ends of doubt in our lives. He wants to show us how far we have yet to go. He wants to show us we are still of "little faith." It may be we have deceived ourselves along the way. Perhaps we've been telling ourselves that we're a man or woman of great faith. But at that dead end of doubt, staring into the teeth of sheer impossibility, we see how far we really have to go.

You could say we experience a faith checkup. We find out where we are in our journey of faith. We learn what the real issues are in our lives and what we need to do about them.

By the way...don't be too hasty to criticize people who are stepping out in faith and venturing for the Lord—even when they stumble, even when they end up thrashing around with a mouthful of seaweed. It's better than staying in the boat and keeping your feet dry!

The only way you're going to grow and mature in your faith is to stand at that place of doubt and fear, reach out your hand toward the Lord's outstretched hand, and take one step—even a baby step—forward. Even if you find yourself going under, He's still there to grab your hand with a grip that cannot be broken.

Obstacles to Faith

"Do not be afraid of them;
remember the Lord who is great and awesome."
NEHEMIAH 4:14, NASB

What are those things that could possibly hinder your faith?

■ **Forgetting you are God's own child.**

For he chose us in him before the creation of the world to be holy and blameless in his sight. In love he predestined us to be adopted as his sons through Jesus Christ, in accordance with his pleasure and will. (Ephesians 1:4–5, NIV)

You are His child. He has chosen you, forgiven you, and accepted you. You belong to Him…you are His personal responsibility.

■ **Forgetting who God is.**

When I become fearful, discouraged, and anxious (and yes, Son, you've seen me like that from time to time), it is usually because I've forgotten who my heavenly Father is.

I've forgotten His power…that He can do anything.

I've forgotten His purpose…that He's up to something in my life.

I've forgotten His presence…that He's always near and wants to help.

I've forgotten His sovereignty…that He's always in control, even when I'm not.

I've forgotten His peace…that exceeds my understanding.

The fact is, helplessness is the first step of faith. The realization of our overpowering need and His total sufficiency is where faith begins.

The Object of Faith

Watch, stand fast in the faith, be brave, be strong.

1 CORINTHIANS 16:13

Sometimes you'll hear people say, "Just have faith."

That's one of those mild, inoffensive clichés almost everyone can repeat. But faith in *what*? Faith in *whom*? We don't put our faith in "faith," but rather in Him who is faithful. We don't put our faith in some vague, foggy concept of a Greater Power, but rather in One who has revealed Himself in the pages of His inerrant Word. For instance, in my study of prayers from the Old Testament, I've seen certain elements appear again and again.

■ **A realization of who God is**

> "O LORD, God of our fathers, are you not the God who is in heaven? You rule over all the kingdoms of the nations. Power and

might are in your hand, and no one can
withstand you." (2 Chronicles 20:6, NIV)

No matter what I'm facing, faith grows when I realize God is the almighty, sovereign Ruler of all. When
I'm not in control, I know He is.

■   **A realization of the things God has done**

"O our God, did you not drive out the inhabi-
tants of this land before your people Israel
and give it forever to the descendants of
Abraham your friend?"
(2 Chronicles 20:7, NIV)

Old Testament saints delighted to rehearse God's
track record, what He accomplished again and again
in the lives of His people. It's encouraging for me to
realize I'm not God's first project—and may not even
be His most troublesome project. I need to rehearse
His works and accomplishments in my memory.

■   **A realization of who I am**

"O our God… We have no power to face
this vast army that is attacking us. We do

not know what to do, but our eyes are upon you." (2 Chronicles 20:12, NIV)

Who am I? I'm a person in constant need. I have very little strength. I frequently don't know what to do or which way to turn. My dependence upon Him is complete.

Faith isn't trying to manipulate God or circumstances to get what I want. It is resting in Him so that I can have what He wants.

Faith isn't feeling; faith is obeying God in spite of feelings and circumstances. When Shadrach, Meshach, and Abednego were sentenced to die by burning because of their refusal to bow before the king's idolatrous image, they may not have "felt good" about their decision. These young men wanted to live as much as any young men want to live. But they chose to obey their God in the face of feelings that might have screamed at them to compromise.

Shadrach, Meshach and Abednego replied to the king, "O Nebuchadnezzar, we do not need to defend ourselves before you in this matter. If we are thrown into the blazing furnace, the God we serve is able to save us from it, and he will rescue us from your hand, O king. But even if he does not, we want you to know, O king, that we will not serve your gods or worship the image of gold you have set up." (Daniel 3:16–18, NIV)

Giving their last full measure of obedience in faith to God, the three young men found the Lord actually standing at their sides in the midst of the flames.

Then King Nebuchadnezzar was aston- ished; and he rose in haste and spoke, say- ing to his counselors, "Did we not cast three men bound into the midst of the fire?" They answered and said to the king, "True, O king."

"Look!" he answered, "I see four men loose, walking in the midst of the fire; and they are not hurt, and the form of the fourth is like the Son of God." (Daniel 3:24–25)

The Activity of Faith

But without faith it is impossible to please Him.

HEBREWS 11:6

Faith always gives you something to do. Here's what I mean by that:

- In Mark 2, when the men lowered the crippled man through the roof so that Jesus might heal him, Scripture says that He "saw their faith" (Mark 2:5).
- Elisha told Naaman the leper, "Go, wash yourself seven times in the Jordan, and your flesh will be restored and you will be cleansed" (2 Kings 5:10, NIV).
- At the wedding in Cana where He turned the water into wine, Jesus told the servants to fill the water pots with water (John 2:7).
- When He fed the five thousand with five loaves and two fish, Jesus commanded the disciples to

have the people sit down in groups of fifty
(Luke 9:14–16).

The lesson? Move out in faith. Step out on
ground that requires God's Spirit to sustain you.
Remove yourself from self-reliance.

Here's a question for you to ponder, Son. In what
areas of your life are you believing God for things
only He could accomplish?

True faith, I believe, is always visible. Please
don't let me hear you say you're "believing God" for
a good marriage. If you tell me you want a happy
home and a great family, then what are you personally doing to show others you mean it? If Jesus lived
in your house (and He does), what would He see you
doing that would convince Him that's what you
deeply desire?

Yes, God will act, but He will ask you to act, too.
If you long for a blessed marriage and family life,
then people ought to see evidence of you tearing up
the roof—cutting a hole through the shingles and
rafters—making room for God to work in the midst
of your home.

If you want to be a person of the Word, then
you'll spend time in the Word.

If you want to be a person of prayer, then you'll spend time on your knees.

If you want to be a compassionate helper, then you'll roll up your sleeves and get after it…doing what you can…trusting God to do what only He can.

The Testing of Faith

*We can be full of joy here and now even in
our trials and troubles. These very things will give
us patient endurance; this in turn will develop a mature
character, and a character of this sort produces
a steady hope, a hope that will never disappoint us.*

ROMANS 5:3–5, *PHILLIPS*

Whenever you find yourself going through times of testing, there is always a reason…a very good reason. In fact, there are several reasons. Let me mention a clever use I've learned for three words that has helped me to remember the value of testing times. Testing times are to:

■ **Uncover something.**
When God allows pressures and trials, it is so that you might uncover something in your life He wants to deal with. Hardships reveal areas of weakness and

vulnerability. God wants to strengthen us in those very areas, and better equip us not only to stand strong in the storms ourselves, but also to be a shelter for others.

■ **Recover something.**

God allows us to be tested so that we might recover something we've lost over the months and years. Perhaps it is our delight in the Word of God, a habit of daily prayer, or the delight of regular fellowship with other believers. Trials may force us back to that "first love" walk with the Lord that has slipped away from us.

■ **Discover something.**

Even though it's a test you may not like or enjoy, you discover that He's your God, you're His child, and He loves you. He'll care for you and see you through.

I hear people talk about this trial and that trial, this test and that test. People will say, "Pray for me, I'm going through a trial in my marriage (or in my job or in my finances or in my relationships at home)."

But in reality, those aren't the things being tested

at all. What's being tested is our faith. What's being tried is our trust in God, whether we will really trust Him to work in and through our circumstances.

That's what's really at stake, Son. When the heat's on…when the shadows fall…when disappointment rips through my heart…am I going to trust Him to do the impossible? Am I going to wait on Him, worship Him, and give my anxieties to Him? Or am I going to turn away from Him in my doubt and discouragement?

The real value of our faith being tried is not to see how we'll respond in a given situation, as much as it is to see how God will respond. We get to stand and watch what He's going to do, in His own way and in His own time.

Growth

Money Matters

Keep your lives free from the love of money and

be content with what you have,

because God has said, "Never will I leave you;

never will I forsake you."

HEBREWS 13:5, NIV

Even at your age, you have probably encountered people whose lives seem to revolve around money. Everything they think about or talk about seems to have dollar signs attached. They measure their lives and success by what they have in the bank or the stock market.

Survey after survey shows that today's young men and women have one great passion. It is getting rich, and they will seemingly do whatever is necessary to succeed. They will sacrifice anything, be it friends or family, to get to the top.

We live in a culture consumed with status and

wealth. You may end up with a bigger house, car, office, a key to the executive washroom, and even your own personalized parking spot. But in the end you'll find that path leads to far more loss than gain.

When I was a boy, one of the first big jobs I had was rolling sod, for a cent and a half a roll. No, that wasn't big pay, but it certainly made me feel rich. In the process, however, I discovered something strange about money. You think you have a lot, and then you look in your pocket or wallet and there's nothing there! You find yourself wondering where it went.

The book of Proverbs tells us that money has wings (Proverbs 23:4–5). One minute it's there, and the next minute it flies away, out of reach. I think that's one of the reasons God admonishes us to lay up treasures in heaven.

With that in mind, I'd like to offer a few suggestions for you to consider:

■ **Live for things that really matter.**
I can't think of any stronger words than the ones Paul used with Timothy:

> People who want to get rich fall into temptation and a trap and into many foolish and

harmful desires that plunge men into ruin
and destruction. (1 Timothy 6:9, NIV)

I'm not saying it's wrong to have extra money or
nice things. I'm talking about the motivational bent of
your life. How you handle your wealth is critical. The
painful scenario Paul painted for his young friend is
repeated over and over by people who refuse to live
by God's principles. The temptation. The trap.
Foolish and harmful desires. Ruin and destruction.
I've seen it too many times through my years of ministry.

■ **Invest in the right place.**

"Do not store up for yourselves treasures on
earth, where moth and rust destroy, and
where thieves break in and steal."
(Matthew 6:19, NIV)

While I know it's important to prepare for the future,
I get concerned when I see people make investments
out of fear…fear that if they don't prepare for tomorrow, they'll have nothing. I'm no financial advisor, but
I think I can appreciate the need to invest in a sure

thing. When you invest with God, it is a sure thing, and it comes with great interest and real dividends.

> "Give, and it will be given to you. A good
> measure, pressed down, shaken together
> and running over, will be poured into your
> lap. For with the measure you use, it will be
> measured to you." (Luke 6:38, NIV)

■ **Don't make wealth your priority.**

> A man with an evil eye hastens after riches,
> and does not consider that poverty will
> come upon him. (Proverbs 28:22)

If your lone motive is to get rich, I doubt God will become too involved in your plans or finances.

■ **Don't be selfish.**

> One man gives freely, yet gains even more;
> another withholds unduly, but comes to
> poverty. (Proverbs 11:24, NIV)

Stinginess will clog the flow of God's goodness. Stingy men are usually regulated by their possessions. If you claim what you have as your own, you'll fight to keep it. *But if you acknowledge that all you have belongs to the Lord, you'll probably be willing to give it away.*

Whenever I think about giving, I'm always drawn to the moving story of the poor widow's offering. We know that she had two tiny copper coins, and both of them put together could purchase absolutely nothing. But the Lord, observing her as she cast the coins into the offering, said she had given more than anyone had. Even though the rich had given huge amounts of money out of their abundance, she gave out of her want and cast in everything she had.

Sometimes, Son, I find myself wondering if giving doesn't really become giving until it *hurts*.

■   Keep your values in order.

He who tills his land will have plenty of bread, but he who follows frivolity will have poverty enough! A faithful man will abound with blessings, but he who hastens to be rich will not go unpunished.
(Proverbs 28:19–20)

Choose carefully the people you are going to follow. Are they only seeking riches? Are they stingy? Those are good guidelines by which to make decisions about leadership.

■   **Don't be deceived by riches.**

> The poor man is hated even by his own neighbor, but the rich has many friends.
> (Proverbs 14:20)

> Wealth brings many friends, but a poor man's friend deserts him.
> (Proverbs 19:4, NIV)

Have you ever noticed that when you have an abundance of money, you also have an abundance of friends? I've never forgotten what happened to heavyweight boxer Mike Tyson. When he became world champion and started raking in his mega-millions, he seemed to have an entourage a mile long. Mike had more pals than he could count.

But then he lost his championship, lost most of his wealth, and had to serve a prison term. When he was set free, where were those friends? Where was that loyal fan club? Where were the buddies and chums hanging on his every word? They were nowhere to be found.

■ **Don't resist God's correction.**

> He who ignores discipline comes to poverty and shame, but whoever heeds correction is honored. (Proverbs 13:18, NIV)

When people aren't doing well, it's usually because they're resistant, if not unwilling, to listen to God's directives. Let me express it like this, by way of an old story. Imagine you're on a scorching hot desert, half-dying of thirst, your lips cracking and your mouth dry as cotton.

Suddenly in front of you, you come upon a pump, and on the top of that pump is a cup of water. You're about to gulp down the water when you see a sign.

The sign reads: *"Greetings, thirsty traveler. Pour this water into the pump to prime it, and you will have all the water you need."*

Would you have faith to do it?

Obeying the Word of God will always seem like

taking a risk…but it's as sure as priming a pump. You may think you're pouring water down the drain, but God's program is sure.

And His kids never go thirsty.

A Few Thoughts About Growth

But my eyes are fixed on you,

O Sovereign LORD; in you I take refuge —

do not give me over to death.

PSALM 141:8, NIV

Artificial things look real but never grow. Real things look real and grow.

And growth can be an uncomfortable proposition at times.

When I was a young teenager, I had growth pains in my legs so intense I couldn't sleep at night. My mom would sometimes sit by my bed and rub my legs to relieve the pain.

Growth means walking around in clothes that no longer fit. It means trading in some of your favorite shirts or slacks or sneakers for new ones that aren't broken in.

Growth means leaving some cherished activities

and interests behind to develop new ones that may seem a little strange at first.

So many people have unrealistic expectations when it comes to God's timing. Don't forget, there is absolutely no such thing as "instant growth." Here are a few thoughts on the subject I'd like to offer you.

■   **Spiritual growth is about *time*.**

Your salvation was not only miraculous, it was instantaneous. Through my years of ministry, I've seen alcoholics, addicts, and prostitutes saved in an instant. I've seen marriages and homes restored in a heartbeat. Praise God for those times! With Him, all things are possible. But generally, that isn't how spiritual growth occurs.

I've heard people say, "God is doing a quick work today." That just isn't true and never will be true. God may be saving people quickly, but He is not maturing people quickly.

A squash may grow in a couple of weeks, but an oak tree matures through many years of sunlight and rain, wind and storm. Which would you prefer your Christian life to resemble?

It just takes time. Yes, I know this all sounds simplistic. But it's important to me that you remember that fact, Son. *It takes time.* So don't be discouraged by how long it seems to be taking to achieve maturity in the Lord. His work in our lives is a process. As Paul wrote, "Being confident of this, that he who began a good work in you will carry it on to completion until the day of Christ Jesus" (Philippians 1:6, NIV).

■ **Spiritual growth is about *focus*.**
Hebrews 12 says we are to look to Jesus, the author and finisher of our faith. That focus is essential. People who look to circumstances for direction or inspiration find nothing to sustain them. But those who look to Jesus remain productive and growing.

In my days as a student athlete, I can remember coaches hollering, "Keep your eyes on the ball, Mehl!" It really didn't matter if it was baseball, football, basketball, golf, or tennis. It was always the same. *"Watch that ball!"*

You can't hit the ball if you don't see it. You can't catch the ball if you don't keep your eye on it. You can't be a great athlete—no matter what sport you choose—without a great amount of focus.

In the same way, keeping your eyes focused and fixed on Jesus Christ as the goal of your life will

always make you a winner. And please remember—
even suffering may be part of that process. Scripture
says that Jesus learned obedience by the things He
suffered (Hebrews 5:8).

■   **Spiritual growth is about *experience*.**

Peter heard the words of Jesus, when He said,
"Without Me you can do nothing" (John 15:5). But
he had to learn the literal truth of that statement
through bitter experience.

Until that occasion, he thought he was strong. He
thought he was loyal. He thought he was a leader. He
thought he was able in his own strength and integrity
to remain steadfast to his Master. But he learned
through his shattering experience of failure just how
much he needed to rely on God rather than himself.

Knowing this, Jesus gave him this charge:
"When you have returned to Me, strengthen your
brethren" (Luke 22:32).

You've probably heard me say it: The Christian
life isn't difficult; it's impossible. Think about this
statement for a moment: *You cannot live the life of God
without the life of God.* You must come to the place
where you know that, without the Lord, you'll never
change.

The following words of Paul are very familiar — but don't let their familiarity rob you of the deep meaning for your life:

> I have been crucified with Christ; it is no longer I who live, but Christ lives in me; and the life which I now live in the flesh I live by faith in the Son of God, who loved me and gave Himself for me.
> (Galatians 2:20)

Growth in your faith, growth in the Lord Jesus, is both gradual and supernatural...so don't give up! As you know, Son, one of Satan's most well-worn tools is discouragement. But just knowing that fact won't keep him from using it on you!

■ **Spiritual growth is about *attitude*.**

The reason some people never grow, never change, is because their basic attitude never changes. They really never learn anything. That's why the children of Israel went around in weary circles for forty years in the wilderness. They walked by the same old rocks, the same old bushes, and the same old stunted trees for four decades, until a whole generation passed away.

You've heard people say, "We've been through this again and again and again. It's the same old thing!" And the sad fact is, they'll keep on going over that old ground until their attitude changes about what God is doing, and they respond to Him in the midst of it.

Two elements are needed to keep life in balance: peace and pressure. When you are too comfortable, the Lord may stir you up, but when you're too pressured, He will arrange a season of rest.

David understood that when he prayed:

You chart the path ahead of me and tell me where to stop and rest. Every moment you know where I am. (Psalm 139:3, TLB)

Whatever season you're in, remember...you're growing.

"I Can Do All Things"

I can do all things through
Him who strengthens me.
PHILIPPIANS 4:13, NASB

Is it true that we are more than conquerors? Is it true we can always prevail, no matter what the odds, no matter what the situation?

The answer is yes.

I can do anything, be ready for anything, and have the strength for anything when I draw that strength from the Lord Jesus Christ.

- I can accomplish all things.
- I can endure all things.
- I can overcome all things.
- I can believe all things.

In Christ, nothing is impossible.

Choosing a Life Partner

A wife of noble character is her husband's crown,

but a disgraceful wife is like decay in his bones.

PROVERBS 12:4, NIV

Choosing a life partner is the biggest decision you'll make outside of choosing to accept Jesus Christ as Savior.

I've met with scores of couples for premarital counseling through the years. And one of the first points I try to get across to them is that "desire" does not equal love.

Desire may be illustrated by a young person who tells you they can't live without you, that they're miserable, and that life seems colorless and empty when you're not around. That may be a form of love, but it's not the sort of love that will hold a marriage together through the years. While they may feel they "need" you today, it's possible that five months from now you'll no longer meet their "need," and they'll find that they "need" someone else.

What I tell these young couples is that love is based on commitment, and that everything you do is to fulfill, satisfy, and serve the one you love. Real love doesn't enter a relationship with an expectation to just receive. It enters a relationship to give and give and give.

Let me illustrate how deceptive the world's definition of "love" can be. Picture a young couple who has been dating for a few weeks. It isn't long before this young man tells his girlfriend how much he loves her and how difficult it is to keep his hands off her. Pressing her to engage in a physical relationship, he explains that he "loves her so much" he can no longer restrain himself.

The truth is, any young woman who hears that line should realize that the young man doesn't love her too much…he loves her too little. Actually, he's not thinking about her. He's only thinking about himself. He would never rob innocence and purity from one he truly loves. His insistence on a physical relationship only proves one thing: he loves himself much more than he loves her.

What really brings peace to a relationship? How
do you choose a marriage partner? Let me leave you
with just a few thoughts.

■ **Make sure your life partner loves God more than he
or she loves you.**

> Jesus replied: "'Love the Lord your God
> with all your heart and with all your soul
> and with all your mind.' This is the first and
> greatest commandment. And the second is
> like it: 'Love your neighbor as yourself.'"
> (Matthew 22:37–39, NIV)

It is so important to observe your partner's love for
God. Why? Because in time, the way he or she loves
and serves Him will be reflected in the way he or she
loves and serves you.

■ **Make sure your life partner is a person of character.**

> Blessed are they whose ways are blameless,
> who walk according to the law of the LORD.
> (Psalm 119:1, NIV)

Men and women of character are trustworthy in all they do and have an appetite for righteousness. They will keep their word no matter what the cost.

■ **Make sure your life partner is kind to others.**

And be kind to one another, tenderhearted, forgiving one another, just as God in Christ forgave you. (Ephesians 4:32)

If you don't see your partner treat others with kindness and grace, in time he or she will be treating you the same way.

■ **Make sure to note the way your life partner dresses.**

And I want women to be modest in their appearance. They should wear decent and appropriate clothing and not draw attention to themselves by the way they fix their hair or by wearing gold or pearls or expensive clothes. For women who claim to be devoted to God should make themselves attractive by the good things they do. (1 Timothy 2:9–10, NLT)

I'm not saying your partner should wear a gunny-sack and combat boots to cover herself. I'm just saying the modest things she wears reveal a lot about her heart.

■ **Make sure your life partner treats his or her parents with honor and respect.**

"Honor your father and mother," which is the first commandment with promise. (Ephesians 6:2)

I have never yet met a young person who is truly successful or blessed who doesn't love his or her parents.

■ **Make sure your life partner is respected by others.**

Choose a good reputation over great riches, for being held in high esteem is better than having silver or gold. (Proverbs 22:1, NLT)

Be wise about how you do this, but I would recommend that you discreetly ask a few people what they have observed about the person you're considering.

Pay as much attention to their hesitations as to their words!

- **Make sure your life partner is not flirtatious.**

  Smooth words may hide a wicked heart,
  just as a pretty glaze covers a common clay
  pot. (Proverbs 26:23, NLT)

A person's actions and looks speak volumes, so be advised, Son, and be wise.

- **Make sure you understand the true priorities of your life partner's life.**

  Don't let anyone think less of you because
  you are young. Be an example to all believers in what you teach, in the way you live,
  in your love, your faith, and your purity.
  (1 Timothy 4:12, NLT)

Watch closely to see signs of your partner's love, faith, and purity. Has this person put God first? Does this person live to serve others? Is this person selfish?

■ **Make sure you know who your life partner's close friends are.**

Do not be misled: "Bad company corrupts good character." (1 Corinthians 15:33, NIV)

■ **Make sure your life partner is not contentious or violent.**

Better a meal of vegetables where there is love than a fattened calf with hatred. (Proverbs 15:17, NIV)

If you're picking up a lot of unhappiness or anger in this person, then be warned in advance.

■ **Make sure you ask the Lord for discernment.**

Show me the way I should go,
for to you I lift up my soul…
May your good Spirit
lead me on level ground.
(Psalm 143:8, 10, NIV)

Trust in the LORD with all your heart; do not depend on your own understanding.

Seek his will in all you do, and he will direct your paths. (Proverbs 3:5–6, NLT)

Make sure you pray, pray, pray.

Show me the path where I should walk, O LORD; point out the right road for me to follow. Lead me by your truth and teach me, for you are the God who saves me. All day long I put my hope in you.
(Psalm 25:4–5, NLT)

Bumps in the Road

Failure

Then Peter remembered the word of the Lord,

how He had said to him, "Before the rooster crows,

you will deny Me three times."

So Peter went out and wept bitterly.

LUKE 22:61-62

Good intentions can only go so far and do so much.

Peter, the disciple, had laudable intentions. He was committed and devoted to Christ. He would eventually be considered the Lord's spokesman and leader of the Twelve. Yet, let's face it. His scorecard was scary reading. His field goals sailed consistently wide of the mark—or never got off the ground. Any coach but Jesus Christ would have sent him to the showers with a one-way ticket home.

In Galilee, he tried to walk on water—and then the sea bottom.

In the Upper Room, he said Jesus would never

wash his feet—and then promptly asked for a bath.

In the hour of his Master's greatest emotional trial—he slept like a guy in a mattress commercial.

At the arrest in the Garden, he flailed about with a sword, delivered a blow to a slave's right ear—and then ran for his life.

In the high priest's courtyard, Peter three times denied even *knowing* Jesus—and then left for a good cry.

Peter didn't want to fail, but he did. Nobody wants to fail. I know you don't. But everybody does. I've never met anyone who deliberately set out to mess up his or her life. I've performed a lot of weddings, but I've never heard anyone say at a ceremony, "Over the next few months, we plan to trash this relationship." I've done a lot of baby dedications, but I've never heard a mom or dad say, "We plan on neglecting this child, or spoiling this child, or for sure alienating this child before she reaches her teens." Most of us are counting on a smooth, freeway ride through life with no speed bumps.

But there are *always* bumps in the road. And they sometimes appear when you least expect them.

After the car wreck of his betrayal, Peter was far from ready to be the keynote speaker on the Day of

Pentecost, and far from ready for the role of martyr that he would ultimately assume.

But he was on his way.

The bewildered apostle may not have realized it at the time, but he was on a journey. Peter had no knowledge of his final destination, so how could he identify landmarks along the way? Only Jesus knew what lay ahead.

Our Lord loves taking us when we have been buried by failure and digging us out. Perhaps, as Jesus looked at Peter in that courtyard, His compassionate eyes were saying, *Peter, I know you're trying, and I know you truly do love Me. You don't know it now, dear friend, but one day you will be called to lay down your life for Me...and you will. You won't run. You won't hide. You won't deny. You will boldly stand, and in the face of death and blood and torture and humiliation, you will own Me as Lord and Christ.*

Jesus knew Peter's denial was not the end but a beginning. He knew that people often fail along life's journey before they succeed.

Before Peter could know the joys of living in victory, he had to admit defeat. He had to acknowledge failure. He had to confess the error of his way.

And so must you and I.

On the road ahead, Son, failures will come. Small ones. Large ones. And all of them grievous. But when you fail, what should you do?

First, confess to the Lord, "I love You."

You'll no doubt rather say you're sorry. Or, "Trust me, Lord, it'll never happen again." But the wisdom of God brings an honest man, a sincere man, one who has failed in his attempt to keep his promise, to something even more painful than the whipping post. For us, like for Peter, it is far more painful and difficult to declare our love and need for the Savior in the face of having so horribly failed Him.

Second, confess to the Lord the truth about yourself: "I have no righteousness of my own. I am only righteous by the blood of Jesus Christ." Or maybe, after reading again Romans 6 through 8, declare, "I am NOT a slave of sin, I am a slave of righteousness. I am NOT under the power of sin, I have been set free. I am NOT a prisoner of my flesh, I can walk every day in the power of the Spirit and in newness of life."

Failure is beyond the power of the enemy. He can assist it, he can attempt to make it happen; he cannot force it. Failure is a product of human effort (see James 1:13–16). Hell will help all it can, but in the final analysis, failure is our responsibility, not Satan's.

And finally, repent.

Repentance is a decision to go another way, to trust the Lord rather than yourself, to admit His way is the right way. The best way to start your journey back to blessing and success is to stop. Stop trying to do it all on your own. Stop making promises to God and to yourself unless you've made a serious decision to rely upon God's power and grace to get it done.

Drastic, radical dependence on Christ is your only hope for success. As someone told me early in my ministry, "God is not obligated to help anyone who isn't totally dependent upon Him."

Thankfully, the Lord has made it easy for you to depend upon Him: He is always available. He is always close by. As certainly as He accompanied Peter on his journey from failure to success, so He will walk with you. He has given you the gift of the Holy Spirit, the One who takes His place "at my side."

And remember: The wonderful thing about knowing Jesus, about being His friend, is that He, and He alone, knows the beginning from the end. He knows His purposes in your life—that they are for good, and for eternity. And He knows that as you cast yourself on His grace and His deliverance, your failure can lead to success.

Loneliness

"Indeed the hour is coming, yes, has now come,
that you will be scattered, each to his own,
and will leave Me alone. And yet I am not alone,
because the Father is with Me."

JOHN 16:32

Counselors tell us that the number one problem plaguing people today isn't fear, insecurity, or rejection. It's loneliness. Isolation. Longing for companionship. I was talking with a woman recently who said, with pain in her eyes, "I've been lonely since I was a little girl. Ever since I can remember, I've felt isolated and alone."

In Psalm 22, David penned what so many of us have felt: "My God, my God, why have you forsaken me? Why do you refuse to help me or even listen to my groans?" (Psalm 22:1, TLB).

If you haven't yet, you'll feel the hard edge of

loneliness at times in the days ahead. A loneliness that makes you cry out with pain, makes you doubt everything you ever held to be true.

Yet David learned something during his lonely times. His message in Psalm 27 contains a perfect kernel of wisdom: "When I'm alone," he says, "and my enemies have come to destroy me, though I'm outnumbered and even my parents have forsaken me, I will wait on the Lord."

As the years have gone by, I've been learning something, too. I've begun to realize that God, my Father, may have had a hand in arranging my lonely seasons, with a good purpose in mind. It is difficult to listen for God's voice in those excruciating moments of lonely isolation. But in every instance when I have genuinely chosen to seek Him in such a season, I have been amply rewarded.

I remember delivering a sermon in one of my classes during my freshman year of Bible college in Los Angeles. I was a young, bashful Midwestern boy, and preaching in front of an indifferent, critical audience turned my insides into jelly.

As it turned out, I had every reason to be apprehensive. My sermon was horrible. An unqualified disaster. When it was over, it seemed as if every member of the class gave a sermon of their own on what I'd done wrong.

I felt like a lonely piece of meat in a bowl filled with piranhas. When they finished chewing on me, it was all I could do to keep from crying.

I walked out of class, stumbled across campus, slipped into the quiet darkness of the college prayer room, and dropped to my knees. I felt sick to my stomach, deeply hurt, and so, so alone.

"Lord," I whispered into the darkness, "You know I want to be a pastor. You know I want to be a preacher, but—I guess I can't preach."

Then, all alone, I heard His voice in my heart as clearly as I'd ever heard it before.

You did well, son. You did your best. You don't need to BE the best. I am pleased with you.

It was during that time alone with the Lord that I realized it was Him I needed to please. It was Him I wanted to honor. During that time alone, I discovered the Lord working something of great value in me. My hunger for ministry grew rather than faded.

So how can you discover the hidden blessings of loneliness?

First, realize that your loneliest moments may be arranged by God. There can be ministry in loneliness.

There can be value in loneliness. If you submit to those times, God will teach you.

Second, decide in advance how you will face those inevitable periods of loneliness and isolation. Do you have three or four people you need to bring before the Lord in prayer? Do you have a couple of areas in your life that continually confuse and frustrate you — things you'd like to spread out before your Father for His counsel? Be ready for lonely moments when they come, and if they don't come, get away by yourself and *find* some.

Third, let your loneliness sensitize you to the heartache of others. Many of us with stable homes and loving church families feel somewhat insulated from the awful emptiness experienced by so many around the world. Sometimes God allows us a taste of that thirst…just to remind us that we are stewards of a full canteen.

Fourth, use those times as a prompt to reach out beyond yourself. Loneliness can be like a silent alarm, reminding you to write that note of encouragement, pick up that phone to call a lonely friend, or walk down the street to visit at a retirement home.

There will never be the slightest current of loneliness blowing through your heart that your loving

Father doesn't see and understand. Before you turn to frantic activity, empty noise, or blank despair, lift your eyes and see if there is something He might want to say to you in those lonely moments.

It may be just what you need to hear.

God's Waiting Room

Wait on the LORD;

Be of good courage,

And He shall strengthen your heart;

Wait, I say, on the LORD!

PSALM 27:14

Waiting isn't likely to make anyone's list of favorite things. Yet the further you venture into adulthood, the more you'll realize that waiting is a rather large and mostly unavoidable chunk of life.

We wait for service in restaurants, counting the holes in the top of the salt shaker. We wait for the traffic to edge forward an inch or two on the way home. We show up fifteen minutes early for our doctor's appointment and end up waiting forty-five minutes—just to get into one of those chilly little examining rooms where we wait for *another* half hour in our underwear.

God has a waiting room, too, you know.

You might not find those exact words in Scripture, but it's there all right. From one end of the Book to the other, God has brought people into the waiting room of delayed dreams.

Can you picture it…that great, celestial waiting room? Can you see it in your mind's eye? One very large room stretching out both ways farther than you can see. Shining floors, marble walls, white-shaded lamps…and countless people sitting in chairs, glancing now and again at the clock on the wall, clearing their throats, drumming their fingers, chewing their lips…and waiting.

Waiting for God to respond.

Waiting for God to keep His promise.

Waiting for God to speak.

Waiting for God to answer.

Waiting for God to heal.

Waiting for God to act.

Can you imagine yourself sitting there…in God's waiting room? You look over to your left and there's Noah, calmly thumbing through a boating magazine. He's waiting for something called "rain." He's never seen it before, but God had said it would come—a lot of it.

Over on your right is Abraham. He's been there a very long time, waiting for a little son whose name would be "Laughter." He's become an old man in that waiting room, but he'll stick it out. He has a promise in his pocket with God's signature on it.

Job is there, too, so weak and doubled over with pain and sorrow he can barely stay in his chair. He's waiting for healing, waiting for a few encouraging words, waiting for someone to help him make sense of a life shattered into a thousand jagged pieces.

Ruth's there, too, waiting for a husband—and a redeemer.

David is there, of course, waiting for a promised kingdom. If you listen carefully, you can hear him pray…

> In the morning, O LORD,
>   you hear my voice;
> in the morning I lay my requests before you
> and wait in expectation.
> (Psalm 5:3, NIV)

One striking young man sits with his hands folded in his lap, his expression alternating between intense longing and sturdy, determined patience. His name is Joseph, and he has spent some of the prime years of his life in God's waiting room.

You probably remember Joseph's story from the book of Genesis. He was sold by jealous brothers into Egyptian slavery, falsely accused by his master's wife, and thrown into the subbasement of an Egyptian prison. He was probably sixteen or seventeen when he was captured, and possibly thirty before he was released.

That's a long time to spend in a waiting room. That's a lot of dreams put on hold.

But while Joseph's dreams were on hold, God was working.

He was working in Israel. He was working in the courts of Egypt. He was working with the weather patterns encircling the globe. He was working in the hearts of Joseph's brothers. And He was working in Joseph's heart, too, refining the young man's faith, drawing him ever closer to the heart of God.

Even though Joseph's plans, hopes, and dreams were waiting, God was not waiting. He was working ceaselessly on His servant's behalf.

At the end of many years, after he had become

ruler of Egypt, Joseph could reflect on those long days and years of waiting and hardship his brothers had put him through, look into their eyes, and say from the heart, "You meant evil against me; but God meant it for good...to save many people alive" (Genesis 50:20). Joseph had held on tight to the promises of God and emerged victorious.

Sometimes I have become so tired of waiting I have wanted to throw in the towel. I suspect you get to that point too. You may come to the point where you find yourself saying, "I can't carry on anymore. I can't believe or trust anymore. In my own strength and in my own wisdom I have nothing left to hope."

But listen: It's at that point, Son—while clinging with all your strength to God—that you are ready to move to another dimension of faith, beyond what seems logical, beyond what makes sense. You are being invited to trust God at a new level. More than ever, He can *become* your hope.

When you're sitting in God's waiting room, remember that you can rely on His love and His promises. Noah did. Abraham did. So did Job, Ruth, David, and Joseph. When He saw that the time was right, God came through for each of them.

You can be sure He'll also come through for you.

A Song in the Dark

Be joyful always.
1 THESSALONIANS 5:16, NIV

The apostle Paul was as specific as he could be when it came to commanding joy in the Christian life:

> Finally, my brothers, rejoice in the Lord!
> …Rejoice in the Lord always. I will say it
> again: Rejoice! (Philippians 3:1; 4:4, NIV)

The only way I know how to live in the reality of these verses—to rejoice all the time, no matter what—is to let your mind dwell on God. People who remain calm and peaceful in the midst of difficult circumstances have a perspective about God that others don't. So many people spend their days looking for quick fixes and Band-Aid solutions to their problems, running everywhere looking for an answer, looking for experiences that will bring a moment or two of happiness.

In commanding joy, Paul never said it would come easy. But you could never accuse the battered apostle of neglecting to practice what he so consistently preached.

In Acts 16, Luke says that Paul and Silas suffered a horrendous beating at the hands of the city fathers of Philippi. Bruised and bleeding, they were locked away in an inner dungeon. The jailer took the precaution of fastening their feet in stocks—an instrument of torture as well as confinement.

Can you imagine the conversation between the prisoners?

"Silas?" Paul whispers. "Silas, are you okay? Is there anything I can do?"

"I'm all right. I'll live, I guess. How about you?"

"I don't think any bones are broken."

"That's a plus, I guess... Paul, what do you think they're gonna do?"

"I don't know, my friend, but it doesn't look good."

"What should we do?"

Paul, a thoughtful man, gives that some consideration. "Remember what our brothers Peter and John did—back in those days when that first wave of persecution hit the church? When the Jewish leaders flogged them, they praised God that they'd been counted worthy to suffer for the sake of the Name. We could do that."

"You mean, just start praising God? Right now? Out loud?"

"Why not?" Paul grins in the dark. "What have we got to lose?"

And so they did. It began with a hoarse whisper and rose to a mighty shout as their joy increased. Soon, they were singing favorite hymns in two-part harmony, full-throated and joyous, in the bowels of that dark place.

Why did they sing? Because they knew that God was going to send an earthquake and open the prison doors for them? No, I don't think they had any idea what God was going to do. Paul and Silas sang expecting nothing. They simply rejoiced because they belonged to the Lord. They sang because they knew their God worked in the dark and that nothing could stand in the way of His purposes.

They didn't sing only for themselves. The sound of their voices drifted along those dark, smelly corridors. The other inmates heard—and must have been stunned by what they were hearing. The wounded men rejoiced, and their rejoicing touched lives.

It's the same for you and me. Never doubt it! No matter what you may be enduring, there are those who will watch and listen to see how you handle it. If there's a song in your heart, when by all reason and logic there shouldn't be, people will listen—and wonder what makes the difference in your life.

Your praise not only touches others, but it also touches the heart of God. And He will not remain idle at such times. He will come to you as He came to Paul and Silas that night in Philippi. When He hears your sacrifice of praise through gray days of pressure or long nights of loneliness and pain, He will do something. I'm not saying that He will immediately open your prison doors or unleash an earthquake, but I believe that your song will activate something in the Almighty, releasing Him to minister in and through you in some fresh and effective way.

A song in the dark is powerful.

A song rising out of sorrow soars like no other.

Dealing with Sin

Temptation

For if, by the trespass of the one man,

death reigned through that one man,

how much more will those who receive God's

abundant provision of grace and of the gift of righteousness

reign in life through the one man, Jesus Christ.

ROMANS 5:17, NIV

My friend Dennis Easter has a unique perspective on temptation.

He says there have been only two kinds of temptation stories since the beginning of time. The temptation of the first Adam in the Garden led to the fall of man. And the temptation of the second Adam, Jesus Christ, led to Satan's fall. All temptation, he says, will conclude with one or the other. Either we will fall as Adam fell, or we will stand as Jesus stood and see Satan fall.

There is no middle ground. There is no other option.

Temptation is always a shortcut. It's Satan's way of offering you now what God wants to give you later on. That's why there is so much premarital sex in our culture these days. Satan says, "You can have it now." What he doesn't tell you is the cost—and the consequences.

Satan says, "I can make you somebody…I can help your image…I can give you the excitement you crave…I can give you power…but you must bow before me now."

Adam went along with that line and began a chain of consequences beyond his imagining. Jesus refused that line and began a chain of consequences that led to our eternal salvation.

Just as Adam decided and Jesus decided, so you too must decide how you will reply to Satan when he comes to entice you with a shortcut.

You might say to me, "Dad, these temptations are awfully strong sometimes. How do I face them?"

Here are a few thoughts I've gleaned through my study.

■ **Remember the promised way of escape.**
Paul wrote,

> No temptation has seized you except what is common to man. And God is faithful; he will not let you be tempted beyond what you can bear. But when you are tempted, he will also provide a way out so that you can stand up under it. (1 Corinthians 10:13, NIV)

There is a way out! There is a way of escape! You and I can stand up under the temptation. Remember that. When the tug toward sin seems irresistible and overpowering, remember that it is neither. The Holy Spirit will supply the escape door if we're truly looking for it.

■ **Cling to strong convictions.**
In times of trial, I discover what I truly believe — not what I say I believe. I find out what I believe about marriage and family, right and wrong, holiness and compromise. You and I can say we're committed, but when we're tempted, we find out if our convictions

are real. As long as we're not faced with the opportunity to sin, we can say whatever we like about how strong and dedicated we are. But until we find ourselves faced with the actual opportunity to be dishonest or to commit adultery or to be caught up in pride, we'll never know how strong those convictions of ours really are.

You can say, "Well, I'd never bow down before an idol no matter what anyone said to me." But until you open your front door and see the soldiers ready to take you away and throw you into a blazing furnace, you don't know how you will respond.

The bottom line: Never depend on your own strength. Humble yourself daily before the Lord. Ask Him to strengthen your faith, strengthen your convictions, and, as Jesus prayed, to lead you not into temptation.

■   **Be a fast runner.**
I read somewhere that when you're fleeing temptation, don't leave a forwarding address! Paul told Timothy:

> Flee the evil desires of youth, and pursue
> righteousness, faith, love and peace, along

with those who call on the Lord out of a
pure heart. (2 Timothy 2:22, NIV)

Run *from* temptation and *to* the Lord. Don't
rationalize...run! Don't walk along the cliff, seeing
how close you can get to the edge...hurry away from
it! You aren't just "running away," you're running to
shelter. You're running to something.

Imagine a World War II bombing run, with
enemy pilots flying in low, dropping bombs and straf-
ing with their machine guns. When the air-raid sirens
go off, you don't just run around in circles. You don't
run laps around the perimeter of the military base.
You run for the air-raid shelter. You run to where you
know there is safety.

The Christian life isn't so much about "dos and
don'ts" as it is about pursuing Jesus Christ, the
author and finisher of your faith. Sometimes someone will say to me, "Pastor, I'm quitting that filthy
habit. I'm not going to do that anymore." When that
happens, I don't look to see what they're running
from, I look to see where they're running to.
Chances are, if you're not running to something,
then you'll probably never run from something.

The truth is, God is more concerned about the direction of your life than the perfection of your life. If you're truly pursuing Him, then God's freeing, perfecting work will follow.

Here's another way to look at it. Let's say you have a temptation to lust after sexual things — something that's pretty common in people your age (or any age, for that matter). Sometimes we entertain those thoughts because we feel an emptiness or restlessness within our spirits. So along comes Satan and offers us thoughts or actions that give us a temporary satisfaction — but then leave us even more empty and restless than before.

Yes, we need to run from such lust. But remember, the thing that made you lust in the first place was the emptiness you felt within. So run to God for the stimulation and satisfaction you need. Let the Spirit lift your spirit and fill you with Himself.

If the temptation is toward drinking, Paul writes, "Do not get drunk on wine, which leads to debauchery. Instead, be filled with the Spirit" (Ephesians 5:18, NIV). Another translation puts it like this: "Don't get your stimulus from wine (for there is always the danger of excessive drinking), but let the Spirit stimulate your souls" (*Phillips*).

■ **Live with patience.**

Our world (taking its lead, I believe, from Satan) always promises quick results. We want our gratification now. We don't want to wait for anything.

The account of Achan in the book of Joshua is the sad story of a man who couldn't wait for God's timing. He took some precious items from the destruction and sacking of Jericho and hid them under the floor of his tent, even though God had said all the spoils of that battle belonged to Him alone. As a result, Israel was defeated in their next battle, and Achan and his whole family met with disaster.

If only Achan had waited.

If only he had denied himself on that fateful day, he would have discovered there were plenty of spoils to go around. The goods and valuables of all the remaining cities the Israelites conquered after that were to be divided among the people. God's provision was abundant and generous. But Achan must have believed Satan's lie: "If you don't take it now, you'll never have it. God wants to keep you from blessing, prosperity, and fulfillment. So you'd better grab it while you can."

A long time ago, Son, someone gave me a piece of advice I've never forgotten. *Don't sacrifice the permanent on the altar of the immediate.*

■   **Live for God and others.**

This thought has been especially helpful to me when I have faced seasons of temptation. I never want to make what might be a significant decision without first asking myself, "What are the consequences going to be for my wife? my boys? my church?"

Consider the effect your decision to succumb to temptation will have on those you love. Jesus certainly modeled that. Everything He did was with you and me in His mind and heart.

■   **Pray.**

This probably should have been *numero uno* on my list. In life, it is always priority number one. In the Gospel of Luke, Jesus said to His disciples, "Pray that you may not enter into temptation" (Luke 22:40).

I think there is reason to put emphasis on the

word *enter* in this verse. The Lord isn't saying, "If you pray, you'll never be tempted." Rather, He is saying, "When temptation comes, pray you won't succumb to it."

The disciples, however, didn't pray. They slept. Then when the crisis was upon them, they deserted their Lord and fled into the night.

■ **Be teachable.**

We can learn from biblical characters, but we can also get an education from those around us. When they give in to temptation, watch to see how painful, expensive, and hard the results are. Resolve to learn from the mistakes of others.

When you think of that old "school of hard knocks," don't let them be *your* hard knocks. Let it be the school of other people's hard knocks! Learn by direct observation, rather than bitter experience. As a pastor, I have vivid memories of the pain and devastation and sorrow people have gone through because of their sin or their neglect. Some of those incidents have been so painful and so "expensive" that I've told myself, "God help me that I will never do that."

There are innumerable illustrations of those who have entered into error and sin—whether athletes, actors and actresses, pastors, or presidents—people who have endured incalculable grief, shame, and loss.

Let me just say this. Don't be foolish enough to think you are a "special case," and that you are some-how immune to falling into the very same sins. You need to learn from the mistakes of others; let them be like big orange warning signs along the highway. When you see them, slow down, take notice, take care, and be very, very cautious.

■   **Respond to the Spirit's promptings.**
Let Him lead you. Stay tuned to His voice. You will hear that "still, small voice" saying to you, "Don't go there. Don't do that. Stay away from that place. Stop what you're doing. Get away from that person. Back out of that situation." When you sense the Spirit of God nudging you, don't wait for a siren, a foghorn, or alarm bells. *Move. Run.* Don't delay.

He will guide you away from danger and harm because He loves you.

When the Holy Spirit speaks to you, you'll have

to make a decision. Deep down, you'll know you have to deal with that voice. Either you will listen to it and respond, or you'll squelch it by saying, "Well, I know He's speaking to me about this matter, but I'm going to ignore Him this time."

He's probably not going to send an angel to tackle you and keep you away from that temptation. He's probably not going to bar the door or strike you with sudden paralysis (although He is certainly capable of dealing with you in any way He pleases). But when you get ready to make a decision to go somewhere, do something, see something, or touch something, and you feel a little spurt of questioning in your heart, then you'd better assume it's the voice of the Holy Spirit. When you suddenly catch a glimpse of the potential ramifications of your actions—a little preview of "coming attractions"—then you'd better assume it's God, counseling you and solemnly warning you in His love.

■ **Keep short accounts with the Lord.**

Here's what I mean. When there is unconfessed sin in your life, even that which seems trivial and small (from your point of view), you are in greater danger of falling into further sin. When you have already disregarded the voice of the Holy Spirit, you will not be able to hear Him speak to you, alerting you to danger.

Ignoring the Spirit's voice has the same effect as putting masking tape over your car's dashboard warning lights. Granted, you will no longer be bothered by those troublesome warnings; but you may also find yourself stranded a long, long way from home.

Walk with Him moment by moment. That's the key. Confess sins as soon as you become aware of them. Don't allow the precious sense of His nearness and presence to fade or be pushed away. When you are enjoying and delighting in His fellowship, you really won't want to turn off the path—and you won't be led astray by Satan's shortcuts or counterfeits. Why embrace a counterfeit when you have the genuine article!

The psalmist wrote:

Because I love your commands more than gold, more than pure gold, and because I consider all your precepts right, I hate every wrong path.
(Psalm 119:127–128, NIV)

■ **Stand on God's Word.**

When Jesus went one-on-one with the tempter in the wilderness, He defeated the adversary by simply quoting the Word of God. In response to three temptations—the lust of the flesh, the lust of the eyes, and the pride of life—Jesus replied, "It is written...," sending the tempter away.

Paul called the Word of God "the sword of the Spirit." And that same Holy Spirit will put a sword in your hand, too, as you memorize the Word and apply it to shoring up the vulnerable areas of your life.

Speaking of vulnerability, I like what Leroy Eims wrote in *Be the Leader You Were Meant to Be*:

> Snakes are fairly common where I live. I encounter one every summer. It's a frightening experience to see a rattlesnake coiled and ready to strike at you. He's lightning quick and accurate. I have a little two-point program for handling rattlesnakes: Shun and Avoid. It's as simple as that. You don't need much insight when it comes to a

diamondback rattler. You just know you
don't mess around.

Jesus taught us to pray, "Lead us not into temptation." In other words, "Lord, give me wisdom to
avoid those areas where I know there are snakes!"

Sowing and Reaping

Do not be deceived: God cannot be mocked.

A man reaps what he sows.

GALATIANS 6:7, NIV

God's creation functions on the basis of laws. It's true in the physical world as well as the spiritual one. You may deny the fact that what goes up must come down, but if you jump out of a second-story window, the law of gravity will take effect…and the landing hurts!

We cannot be indifferent to or ignore the laws of God. He tells us very clearly that what we sow, we will also reap.

> The one who sows to please his sinful
> nature, from that nature will reap destruc-
> tion; the one who sows to please the Spirit,
> from the Spirit will reap eternal life. Let us

not become weary in doing good, for at the
proper time we will reap a harvest if we do
not give up. (Galatians 6:8–9, NIV)

I find that at least half the problems I encounter
during marital counseling sessions were sown during
premarital relationship days. Long before they said
their vows, these couples were planting seeds that
would sprout in the new soil of the marriage.

God's laws of sowing and reaping are fixed; you
cannot ignore them without paying a price. I have
grown up hearing about the sexual revolution and the
concept of "free love." Yet in every counseling situation with young people who have involved themselves in immorality, there has been a price to pay.
And sometimes a terrible one.

Let me make the modest suggestion that you
engrave the following "laws of the harvest" on your
spiritual forehead!

■ **Everyone will reap exactly what he sows.**
It seems that it is always easier to grow weeds than it
is to grow vegetables. My mom taught me that if you
plant corn, you get corn. If you plant potatoes, you
harvest spuds and only spuds...not cantaloupes, not

peaches, not turnips. Please remember that your choices will determine your harvest.

> "If you give, you will receive. Your gift will
> return to you in full measure, pressed down,
> shaken together to make room for more,
> and running over. Whatever measure you
> use in giving—large or small—it will be
> used to measure what is given back to you."
> (Luke 6:38, NLT)

I've always heard this passage taught in the context of giving. But the more I look at it, the more I see a larger context, involving how you and I treat people. The "giving" isn't just about giving money; it's about loving, about doing good, about compassion, about forgiving, about not judging or criticizing others. And the message (again) is that *you will reap exactly what you sow*.

If you are a forgiving person, then people will find it easy to forgive you. If you are patient with people, they'll be patient with you. If, on the other hand, you are a critical, mean, unkind person, you will find yourself disliked, criticized, and treated with coolness.

■ **Everyone will reap in proportion to what he has sown.**

> Remember this: Whoever sows sparingly
> will also reap sparingly, and whoever sows
> generously will also reap generously.
> (2 Corinthians 9:6, NIV)

This certainly has to do with the stewardship of our monies; God seems to suggest that our money is a type of seed. The *attitude* behind the sowing of that seed will determine how much we reap.

■ **Everyone will reap much more than he sows.**

If you plant an apple seed, you get a tree full of apples. But what's that old saying? "You can count the seeds in an apple, but you can't count how many apples there are in a seed." A young man who chooses to watch a pornographic movie to satisfy a desire will find that those visual images have left seeds that will begin to grow in his mind. He may eventually find himself in the grip of lustful passion greater than he ever imagined. And that which he was only intending to "toy with" in his mind becomes an insatiable tyrant that enslaves him.

■ **Everyone should be careful about what he sows.**
Paul warns us in Galatians 6 that if you plant a seed in the soil of flesh, you will reap corruption and a harvest that won't last. It will fade away.

■ **Everyone will reap in a later season than they've sown.**
I've heard young people call this teaching on sowing and reaping hogwash (or worse) right to my face. They will say, "Look at me. I've sown to the flesh. I've done what I wanted to do. But I'm not reaping anything. I've gone my own way and look at me. I'm fine."

What does the Scripture say? *"God is not mocked."* It means no one can snub or turn up his or her nose at God. You will reap, usually at a later date, and often when you least expect it.

No one tried to cover his sin more than David. But it didn't work, did it? Not only was it revealed to the whole kingdom, it was revealed to the ages...down to this very day. The fact is, you cannot tolerate sin in one area of your life and expect to be victorious in other areas. You can't sow to the flesh and then pray for a crop failure.

But this law also applies on the positive side of the ledger. Scripture says, "Do not grow weary in doing good" (2 Thessalonians 3:13). Even when there seem to be no results, *don't quit*. If you are teaching a Sunday school class and it doesn't grow, *stick with it*. If you show love to someone and there's no love shown in return, *don't stop*.

Sow those good words, those good actions in the name of Jesus. In due season...in His time...you'll reap a wonderful harvest.

Forgiveness

And forgive us our debts,

as we forgive our debtors.

MATTHEW 6:12

The New Testament word for *forgive* means "to send away."

And that's what God does with our sins when we have trusted Jesus Christ for salvation. He sends our sins away. On the cross, He sent those sins upon His own Son, the One who "became sin for us."

In forgiveness, the innocent party always pays. I sinned…Jesus died.

Prior to the cross, obtaining God's forgiveness was an uncomfortable business. It was costly, embarrassing, and shameful. In that society, you had to buy an animal for sacrifice and then go see the priest. As you took your sacrifice to the temple to offer it up as an offering for sin, most everyone knew what you had done; they could tell by what you were offering. No matter if it was a turtledove, a bull, or a lamb, people would see the animal and speculate about your transgression. The neighbors would say, "Ah, there goes ol' Jethro up to the priest. He's done it again."

True forgiveness, however, is found in Jesus Christ. He paid the price. He Himself endured the shame…walked through the streets in disgrace…submitted Himself to the mocking and scorn…shed His own blood. And only He can say, "Your sins be forgiven you."

Even on a personal, horizontal level, forgiveness doesn't come from me; it comes from Him. I forgive others because He has forgiven me.

I once heard a moving story about Joe Paterno, longtime football coach at Penn State University. The Nittany Lions were playing for the national championship. They scored a touchdown to win the game, with no time on the clock, sending their fans into pandemonium. But to the dismay of the blue and white, the touchdown was called back. The officials called a penalty on Penn State for having twelve players on the field.

After the game, the media swarmed Paterno.

"Who was that guy?" they demanded. "Who was that twelfth man?"

Paterno said, "Listen, gentlemen, I have no intention of ever identifying the boy. He just made a mistake. There are only two people who know, and I won't tell." That's forgiveness.

You can't give forgiveness horizontally until you have appropriated forgiveness vertically. I can try to forgive someone from the heart, but true forgiveness comes when I look to God and realize He's the One who gives the power to forgive.

Someday, you may hear someone say, "I just can't find it in me to forgive this person." And you can reply, "That's so true. You can't find it 'in yourself' because it isn't there! The power to forgive comes from the Lord."

Remember that no matter how much of God's forgiveness and love you have received, there's still more.

Forgiveness is the greatest act of God. He created the universe with a word (Psalm 33:6). He said,

"Let there be light." He spoke, and the star-studded reaches of space leaped into being. It wasn't a "big bang"; it was a simple word.

But He could not in the same way say, "Let there be forgiveness of sins." No, there was a price to be paid. He had to sacrifice His only begotten Son, even Jesus, to accomplish salvation. Scripture says of Jesus that He was "the Lamb slain from the foundation of the world" (Revelation 13:8).

Every human being's greatest need is forgiveness of sins. "For all have sinned and fall short of the glory of God" (Romans 3:23). I have. You have. Our only hope for eternal life is to receive God's forgiveness (John 3:16). That is the experience all of us need more than any other.

But every soul who is forgiven must also be forgiving. *No one is ever more like God than when he or she is forgiving.* Jesus insisted that we forgive—and not only in the Lord's prayer.

> "And whenever you stand praying, if you
> have anything against anyone, forgive him,
> that your Father in heaven may also forgive
> you your trespasses. But if you do not for-

give, neither will your Father in heaven forgive your trespasses." (Mark 11:25–26)

Then Peter came to Him and said, "Lord,
how often shall my brother sin against me,
and I forgive him? Up to seven times?"
Jesus said to him, "I do not say to you, up to
seven times, but up to seventy times seven."
[In other words, without limit.]
(Matthew 18:21–22)

Forgiving all who have wronged you is
extremely important to God because He knows that
unforgiveness will steal your joy and make you miserable.

The Effects of Sin

"See, you have been made well.
Sin no more lest a worst thing come upon you."

JOHN 5:14

Failure occurs for basically two reasons: human weakness and sin.

Weakness is simply a fact of life. We're human. We fail because we are imperfect, inadequate, finite beings with glaring limitations. We are limited in our strength, in knowledge, and in understanding.

Scripture makes it clear God understands our weaknesses.

> For He Himself knows our frame; He is mindful that we are but dust.
> (Psalm 103:14, NASB)

But sin isn't just weakness; it's willfulness. How does sin happen?

■ **Sin happens when we miss the mark.**
It is failing to do what God wants us to do and failing
to be what God wants us to be. Like an arrow that
falls short of the target and buries itself in the dirt, so
you and I miss God's standards.

■ **Sin happens when we knowingly disobey God's
commands.**
This occurs when I know very well what is right, but
deliberately and willfully step across the line and do
what is wrong.

■ **Sin happens when I slip across the line.**
Sometimes, in a careless, unguarded moment, I stray
in my thoughts, words, or actions, and fall flat on my
face. It's like stepping on an icy porch or sidewalk
and losing my balance. It's not as calculated as delib-
erate disobedience…but it's still sin.

Do you remember reading literary classic *Gulliver's
Travels* by Jonathan Swift? In the book, Gulliver
ends up on an island where he is surrounded by tiny
people called Lilliputians, each only six inches tall.
Those little folks—even their full army—have no

power to conquer a full-grown man like Mr. Gulliver. But in an unguarded moment, "the giant" falls asleep. As he slumbers, the Lilliputians begin to stretch small strands of twine over his body. Back and forth, back and forth they work, until his body was covered.

One, two, three, or even a dozen strands could never have held Gulliver. But many such strands, tiny as they were, bound him fast. And so it is with repeated, habitual sin.

The lesson, Son, couldn't be more simple. Stay alert to the deceptive power of sin in your life. Don't allow yourself to be bound.

This quote was in my mother's Bible. The longer I've lived, the more I've seen it proven true.

Sin will take you farther than you want to go.
Sin will cost you more than you want to pay.
Sin will keep you longer than you want to stay.

One Man's Testimony

For day and night Your hand was heavy upon me;

my vitality was drained away as with

the fever heat of summer.

PSALM 32:4, NASB

When it comes to the effects and consequences of sin, I know of no better life to study than that of David.

Psalm 51 is the heart-cry of a broken, repentant man. Remember what I said earlier, Son, about how Wisdom cries out in the street—how the grief and consequences of those who have sinned can warn us and instruct us?

With that thought in mind, this psalm would be a wonderful portion of Scripture to memorize. Here are a few of the important thoughts it contains.

■ **Sin makes you feel dirty.**

> Have mercy upon me, O God,
> According to Your lovingkindness;
> According to the multitude of
>   Your tender mercies,
> Blot out my transgressions.
> Wash me thoroughly from my iniquity,
> And cleanse me from my sin. (vv. 1–2)

King David may have bathed in a marble tub and slept on silk sheets, but after his sin with Bathsheba, he felt soiled. He cried out, "O God, cleanse me!"

That's one way to determine whether you are truly a child of God. Ask yourself, *When I sin, do I feel unclean? Do I feel guilty?* Those outside of Christ may not feel anything after they sin—unless it's regret after being caught. David, however, knew his soul was deeply stained. He cried out to God for cleansing.

■ **Sin affects your mind.**

> For I acknowledge my transgressions,
> And my sin is always before me. (v. 3)

David's mind was bombarded every day by what he had done. He said, "It's always before me. I can't get away from it!" A nonbeliever, you see, can forget his or her sin. But a Christian can never forget unconfessed sin, because the Holy Spirit won't allow it. It so affects your mind that when you call out to God, you'll feel as though you "can't get through."

Sin will drain you of all confidence before Him. You'll find yourself asking, *Why should God hear or answer my prayer after what I've done?* It's a worthwhile question because Scripture clearly teaches that "if I regard iniquity in my heart, the Lord will not hear" (Psalm 66:18).

■ **Sin will break you emotionally.**

> Make me hear joy and gladness,
> That the bones You have broken may rejoice.
> (v. 8)

Some people say sin is like going to Disneyland. You can ride the rides as long as you like, over and over, and never pay. Wrong!

If you've ever experienced it, you know that there is nothing that hurts quite as much as a shattered bone. And that's the term David used to describe the internal pain he felt. "Lord, You're breaking my bones!" Today we might say, "I feel crushed."

When you sin, God doesn't throw you away; He holds onto you…and just squeezes you harder! He will do anything to keep the pressure on you, until you return to Him with a truly broken heart.

■ **Sin will steal your joy.**

> Restore to me the joy of Your salvation,
> And uphold me by Your generous Spirit.
> (v. 12)

David was thoroughly miserable. Why? Because the most unhappy person in the world is not a lost individual, but a believer who is living in sin. David didn't say, "Restore to me my salvation," because he had never lost it. He said, "Restore to me the *joy* of my salvation." He *had* lost that!

Some say, "Well, you can't be happy all the time." That may be true, but I'm really not talking about happiness. Happiness is based on what happens in your life. If things are going well, if the skies are blue and you have money in the bank, you're happy.

Joy, however, is rejoicing in the Lord always. It's a much more profound state of being, akin to the deep waters of a lake that can't be disturbed by surface winds. And the one thing that can rob that deep-down joy faster than anything else is sin.

■ Sin affects your witness.

> Save me from bloodguilt, O God,
> the God who saves me,
> and my tongue will sing of
>   your righteousness.
> O Lord, open my lips,
> and my mouth will
>   declare your praise.
> (vv. 14–15, NIV)

David, "the sweet psalmist of Israel" (2 Samuel 23:1), hadn't been singing. There was no music in his soul, no tune on his lips, no praise in his mouth. He was a bitterly unhappy man. Those who had known him for years must have whispered in private, "Something's different. David's changed. He's not the man he used to be."

No one was moved toward God by David's

devotion or his praise any longer. The unhappy man's witness for the Lord was zero.

There is only one way to have a life that gives glory to God, and that's by dealing with sin. Let's talk about that...on the next page.

How to Deal with Sin

I acknowledged my sin to You,
and my iniquity I have not hidden.
I said, "I will confess my transgressions to the LORD,"
and You forgave the iniquity of my sin.

PSALM 32:5

There is more, much more to be gleaned from Psalm 51, King David's great psalm of confession and repentance.

We've considered the effects of sin in the previous few pages. Let me take just a moment with you to consider how to confront sin in your life.

■ **Ask for forgiveness.**

Have mercy upon me, O God,
According to Your lovingkindness;
According to the multitude of
    Your tender mercies,
Blot out my transgressions. (v. 1)

One of David's best traits was his willingness to repent. First John 1:9 says, "If we confess our sins." That suggests we know what they are. But David went even further than that. He would pray, "Lord, search me, try me. See if there's anything I'm missing."

■   **Agree with God about your sin.**

> For I know my transgressions,
> and my sin is always before me.
> Against you, you only, have I sinned
> and done what is evil in your sight,
> so that you are proved right
>   when you speak
> and justified when you judge. (vv. 3–4, NIV)

In our world today, it seems everyone is the "victim," and no one wants to take responsibility. David, however, made no excuses. He looked at his sin and said the same thing God says about it.

■   **Accept cleansing.**

> Purify me from my sins, and I will be clean;
> wash me, and I will be whiter than snow.
> (v. 7, NLT)

I love the story of the poor woman who walked for miles to the river to wash her clothes. When she arrived at the riverbank, she noticed a large number of people who were also washing their clothes. Embarrassed by the worn, tattered condition of her garments, she wouldn't even open her bag. Instead, she just dipped the whole bundle into the water and pulled it out again. The woman's laundry got wet…but it wasn't clean.

If you come to God's cleansing stream and, as David did, spread it all out before the Lord in confession and repentance, He will wash away all your sins. You'll rise from your knees with a clean heart.

I'm thinking ahead, Son, to those days when I can't be there. Remember to deal with sin in your life as soon as you become aware of it. Don't lay your head on your pillow at night with unconfessed sin on your conscience.

I know of no better aid to a good night's sleep than a clean conscience.

Ten Things I've Learned

*But your iniquities have separated
you from your God; and your sins have hidden
His face from you, so that He will not hear.*

ISAIAH 59:2

- Sin is like cancer; if it isn't dealt with, it spreads.
- Sin is hard work.
- Sin always means settling for second best (no matter what Satan tells you).
- Sin won't stop God from giving, but it will stop you from receiving (just ask Adam and Eve).
- Sin is setting out to meet your own needs.
- Sin is showing utter disregard for God's law.
- Sin is disobeying God's voice.
- Sin produces bondage.
- Sin causes others to stumble.
- Sin short-circuits our prayers.

If I had cherished sin in my heart, the Lord
would not have listened; but God has surely
listened and heard my voice in prayer.
(Psalm 66:18–19, NIV)

Concluding Thoughts

What We All Need

But God demonstrates His own love toward us,
in that while we were still sinners, Christ died for us.

ROMANS 5:8

■ **We need to be led.**

God never intended for us to lead ourselves. He knows us. He knows we lack direction and stamina. He knows how often we lose our way, become weary, or fall into traps. How He longs to lead us! All we have to do is listen for His voice.

> But when He saw the multitudes, He was moved with compassion for them, because they were weary and scattered, like sheep having no shepherd. (Matthew 9:36)

> He leads me beside the still waters. He restores my soul; He leads me in the paths

of righteousness for His name's sake.
(Psalm 23:2–3)

■   **We need to be protected.**

Apart from God's help, we are extremely
vulnerable in this fallen world; yet we seem
prone to wandering away from His protec-
tion and care. No matter where you are or
where you go, you can say, like Peter,
"[I am] kept by the power of God"
(1 Peter 1:5).

"So they were scattered because there was
no shepherd; and they became food for all
the beasts of the field when they were scattered. My sheep wandered through all the
mountains, and on every high hill; yes, My
flock was scattered over the whole face of
the earth, and no one was seeking them or
searching for them."
(Ezekiel 34:5–6)

■ **We need to be healed.**

Whether it's physically, emotionally, or spiritually, we all have wounds, injuries, and illnesses that need His touch. There's no physician like the Great Physician. Because He created us, He knows us. He can examine us and knows what's wrong in a minute. And He knows just what remedy is needed.

> And when Jesus went out He saw a great multitude; and He was moved with compassion for them, and healed their sick.
> (Matthew 14:14)

■ **We need to be taught.**

We learn through the Word of God, as the Holy Spirit illuminates our understanding. We learn through our experiences, as our indwelling Counselor and Teacher helps us interpret our circumstances and gives us His perspective. And we learn wisdom by observing the lives of others—both those who have turned from God's ways and suffered the consequences, and those who have embraced His ways and enjoy His blessing and favor.

The people were amazed at his teaching,
because he taught them as one who had
authority, not as the teachers of the law.
(Mark 1:22, NIV)

"But the Helper, the Holy Spirit, whom the
Father will send in My name, He will teach
you all things, and bring to your remem-
brance all things that I said to you."
(John 14:26)

This is what we speak, not in words taught
us by human wisdom but in words taught
by the Spirit, expressing spiritual truths in
spiritual words. (1 Corinthians 2:13, NIV)

■   **We need to be fed.**

God promises daily bread and provision for our soul.
God knows that the hunger we have can only truly
be satisfied by Him.

"I am the LORD your God, who brought
you up out of Egypt. Open wide your

mouth and I will fill it.... If my people
would but listen to me, if Israel would follow my ways.... But you would be fed with
the finest of wheat; with honey from the
rock I would satisfy you."
(Psalm 81:10, 13, 16, NIV)

Jesus said to them, "I am the bread of life.
He who comes to Me shall never hunger,
and he who believes in Me shall never
thirst." (John 6:35)

And my God shall supply all your need
according to His riches in glory by Christ
Jesus. (Philippians 4:19)

A Few Thoughts on Prayer

Rejoicing in hope, patient in tribulation,

continuing steadfastly in prayer.

ROMANS 12:12

◼ **Prayer isn't asking for things from God, but asking things for God.**

"Your kingdom come, your will be done on earth as it is in heaven."
(Matthew 6:10, NIV)

◼ **Prayer isn't using God to accomplish your goals, but letting Him use you to accomplish His.**

Then I heard the voice of the Lord saying, "Whom shall I send? And who will go for us?" And I said, "Here am I. Send me!"

He said, "Go and tell this people…"
(Isaiah 6:8–9, NIV)

■ **Prayer is a sure cure for anxiety.**

Do not be anxious about anything, but in
everything, by prayer and petition, with
thanksgiving, present your requests to God.
And the peace of God, which transcends all
understanding, will guard your hearts and
your minds in Christ Jesus.
(Philippians 4:6–7, NIV)

■ **Prayer is the first step to meeting any challenge.**

However, the report went around concern-
ing Him all the more; and great multitudes
came together to hear, and to be healed by
Him of their infirmities. So He Himself
often withdrew into the wilderness and
prayed. (Luke 5:15–16)

■   **Prayer is a remedy for weariness and discouragement.**

Then He spoke a parable to them, that men
always ought to pray and not lose heart.
(Luke 18:1)

■   **Prayer is the best cure for temptation's urges.**

He said to them, "Pray that you may not
enter into temptation." (Luke 22:40)

"Keep watching and praying that you may
not come into temptation; the spirit is willing, but the flesh is weak."
(Mark 14:38, NASB)

■   **Pray in the morning, before temptation rears its head.**

My voice You shall hear in the morning,
    O LORD;
In the morning I will direct it to You,
    and I will look up.
For You are not a God who takes pleasure
    in wickedness,
Nor shall evil dwell with You.
(Psalm 5:3–4)

■ **Prayer is a time of reminding yourself who God is and what He's done.**

When I consider your heavens, the work of your fingers, the moon and the stars, which you have set in place, what is man that you are mindful of him? (Psalm 8:3–4, NIV)

■ **Prayer reminds you that, while you may be flustered and afraid, God is not.**

You will keep him in perfect peace, whose mind is stayed on You, because he trusts in You. (Isaiah 26:3)

■ **Prayer should be a lifestyle, not an event.**

Rejoice always, pray without ceasing, in everything give thanks; for this is the will of God in Christ Jesus for you. (1 Thessalonians 5:16–18)

■ **The purpose of prayer is not to educate God. He already knows everything.**

"And when you are praying, do not use meaningless repetition as the Gentiles do, for they suppose that they will be heard for their many words.

"So do not be like them; for your Father knows what you need before you ask Him." (Matthew 6:7–8, NASB)

■ **Prayer should be based on God's Word.**

They raised their voices together in prayer to God. "Sovereign Lord," they said, "you made the heaven and the earth and the sea, and everything in them. You spoke by the Holy Spirit through the mouth of your servant, our father David." (Acts 4:24–25, NIV)

■ **Prayer releases the power of God.**

Therefore confess your sins to each other and pray for each other so that you may be healed. The prayer of a righteous man is powerful and effective. (James 5:16, NIV)

■ **Prayer will lighten your load.**

But they that wait upon the LORD shall renew their strength; they shall mount up

with wings as eagles; they shall run, and not
be weary; and they shall walk, and not
faint. (Isaiah 40:31, KJV)

Four Things to Remember

Are not five sparrows sold for two pennies?

Yet not one of them is forgotten by God.

Indeed, the very hairs of your head are all numbered.

Don't be afraid; you are worth more than many sparrows.

LUKE 12:6–7, NIV

■ **There is nothing God doesn't know.**

Oh, the depth of the riches of the wisdom
and knowledge of God! How unsearchable
his judgments, and his paths beyond tracing
out! (Romans 11:33, NIV)

Nothing is too complex for Him, nothing is too
involved for Him, and nothing is too difficult or perplexing for Him. When it comes to your life, He
knows *everything*. He knows you, knows where you
are, knows what you're feeling, and knows what

you're going through. He knows everything that happened yesterday and everything that's going to happen tomorrow.

■ **There is nothing God doesn't see.**

"Can anyone hide in secret places so that I cannot see him?" declares the LORD. "Do not I fill heaven and earth?" declares the LORD. (Jeremiah 23:24, NIV)

The night might be dark...the circumstances might be tangled and confused...the deception might be heavy...fog and mist might settle over everything, and you may not feel that you can see beyond the end of your nose. But there is nothing that escapes the Lord's notice. And if you take His hand, He will guide you and keep you from stumbling.

■ **There is nothing God doesn't hear.**

I have called upon You,
    for You will hear me, O God;
Incline Your ear to me, and hear my speech.
(Psalm 17:6)

He inclines—bends way over—to hear your briefest thought or faintest whisper. The Spirit of God can even translate the sighs or groanings of your heart when you can't put two words together. It doesn't matter where you are—the bottom of a well or the dark side of the moon—He hears you when you call.

After you are gone from here in a life of your own, it's important to me that you remember that.

■ **There is nothing God can't do.**

> Surely the arm of the LORD is not too short to save. (Isaiah 59:1, NIV)

> "Ah, Sovereign LORD, you have made the heavens and the earth by your great power and outstretched arm. Nothing is too hard for you." (Jeremiah 32:17, NIV)

There is nothing He can't accomplish. Nothing He can't fix. Nothing He can't forgive. You can trust Him with your problems, your anxieties, your worries about the future, your life, and your eternity.

Am I Doing the Right Thing?

Show me your ways, O LORD, teach me your paths;

guide me in your truth and teach me,

for you are God my Savior,

and my hope is in you all day long.

PSALM 25:4-5, NIV

There's more...and more and more and more. Because when you walk with the Lord, you never exhaust the supply of His Spirit or learn the depths of His love. My desire is that you'll always choose to walk in the Spirit. Remember, choosing to walk in the Spirit means choosing *not* to walk in the flesh.

We all wonder from time to time if what we're doing is right. The following simple questions might help you feel good about your choices.

■ Is this biblical?

Does God's Word give you the freedom and the right? Does what you're about to do have His approval? When you're confused, you will discover you know what *not* to do by knowing what *to* do.

■ Is it helpful?

Will what you're about to do help you grow? Will it help you down the path of God's purpose for your life?

■ Is it what Jesus would do?

When I would ask my mom if I could do something I knew was borderline or debatable, she'd say, "Well, son, is that what Jesus would do? Is that where Jesus would go?"

■ Is it necessary?

Who is really in control of your life? Ask yourself if you can say yes or no to this decision. Do you *have* to do it? If you are in control, then you can say yes or no. The fact that others are doing it (and putting you under pressure to do it, too) doesn't make it right.

■ Is it wise?

Make sure you consider the consequences before you do this. Sin always pays a wage. And even though we love you, Son, you're not exempt from this principle.

■ Is it profitable?

How will what you're about to do affect your testimony? You should desire to grow and mature but also be concerned about others.

■ Is it essential?

Many people carve out enormous periods of time for things that hold little value.

■ Is it the right choice?

It's important to make sure that what you're about to do is biblical, helpful, necessary, and wise. But the greater concern is this: Even after you know those things, will you still choose to do it? Many know what's right but still choose what's wrong. One of the things I love about you, Son, is that I know you'll do what's right.

Choosing the pathway of right choices, though it is often steep and frequently narrow, will give you a deep, abiding sense of purpose and an unshakable joy.

Besides that, it's a path that's really going somewhere. And there's no human tongue that can describe the wonders that await, just over the horizon.

Thinking About Heaven

As it is written: "No eye has seen,
no ear has heard, no mind has conceived
what God has prepared for those who love him."

1 CORINTHIANS 2:9, NIV

"All good things," they say, "must come to an end."
But it isn't true. In fact, the very best things never
end. Heaven, our eventual home, is a blessing that
will last forever.

Our fellowship with the Lord will never end.

Our enjoyment of one another will never end.

Our joy and gladness of heart will never end.

Our service to the King of kings will never end.

The excitement and adventure of exploring the
unimaginable splendors and beauty of our new home
will never, ever end.

As with so many things of spiritual and lasting
value, the concept of heaven is mocked and distorted
by our culture. We lump it together with jokes about

St. Peter and populate it in our minds with puffy white clouds, cute little angels, and bored-looking people walking around in bathrobes. It's been called "a legendary land that never was, with lakes of lemonade and ham sandwich trees." Some people dismiss it as "pie in the sky, by and by." But Jesus taught otherwise. He proclaimed heaven as a real place. He promised His disciples:

> "Do not let your heart be troubled…in My Father's house are many dwelling places; if it were not so, I would have told you; for I go to prepare a place for you. If I go and prepare a place for you, I will come again and receive you to Myself, that where I am, there you may be also."
> (John 14:1–3, NASB)

The place our Lord has prepared is far more splendid than any place where our family—or any family—has ever lived on earth. Scripture speaks of streets of transparent gold, gates of pearl, and walls of jasper embedded with gems flashing all the colors of the rainbow. The most beautiful vistas on earth—whether soaring mountains, crashing seas, or vast fields of golden grain rippling in the wind—are only *shadows* of what will be.

The apostle John extolled such wonders in the last two chapters of the Bible. As you read that elderly disciple's account, you sense him struggling to put it into words. The very heart of all the wonders of heaven, however, is Jesus Christ Himself.

Jesus will be there in our Father's house.

He waits for us even now—this very minute.

There's an old song that says, "Where Jesus is, 'tis heaven." Without Him, the splendors would be just empty sightseeing.

The deepest longing of my heart, Son, is that our whole family will be together eternally in heaven.

You've probably heard someone being criticized as "too heavenly minded to be of any earthly good." But I don't think that's our problem these days. I think we're much too earthly minded—and miss a great deal of heavenly good!

Our minds are so often wrapped up with and preoccupied by that which is temporary and must pass away. We worry about things that, in the long run, don't really matter at all. We become heavy-hearted and discouraged. We lose our perspective and seemingly lose our way.

I recommend that you develop the habit of thinking about heaven. Have you ever found yourself looking forward to a trip or a vacation? Just the thought of where you'll be or what you'll be doing or whom you'll be with can lift your heart, can't it? It can help you get through some of the dry times. It can give you that little surge of anticipation.

Why should it be any different with heaven?

Heaven is a true place and the true destination of all who have been purchased by the blood of Jesus Christ. Jesus Himself has made our reservations and is personally preparing our accommodations. (Can you even imagine that?) Our stay in heaven won't rush quickly by like a nice vacation; it will never end.

With these thoughts in mind, I sat back in my chair here in my office and tried to recall some of the things I've said and heard about why keeping heaven in view can change your life.

■ **Thinking about heaven will remind you of people you love who are already there.**

The dead in Christ will rise first. After that, we who are still alive and are left will

be caught up together with them in the
clouds to meet the Lord in the air. And so
we will be with the Lord forever.
(1 Thessalonians 4:16–17, NIV)

■ **Thinking about heaven will heal you of carnal living.**

Set your minds on things above, not on
earthly things. For you died, and your life is
now hidden with Christ in God. When
Christ, who is your life, appears, then you
also will appear with him in glory.

Put to death, therefore, whatever
belongs to your earthly nature: sexual
immorality, impurity, lust, evil desires and
greed. (Colossians 3:2–5, NIV)

■ **Thinking about heaven will bring joy to your heart.**

Surely goodness and love will follow me all
the days of my life, and I will dwell in the
house of the LORD forever.
(Psalm 23:6, NIV)

■ **Thinking about heaven will help you persevere and keep your commitments.**

I have fought the good fight, I have finished the race, I have kept the faith. Finally, there is laid up for me the crown of righteousness, which the Lord, the righteous Judge, will give to me on that Day, and not to me only but also to all who have loved His appearing. (2 Timothy 4:7–8)

■ **Thinking about heaven will remind you where to invest—time, talents, and treasure.**

"Do not lay up for yourselves treasures on earth, where moth and rust destroy and where thieves break in and steal; but lay up for yourselves treasures in heaven…for where your treasure is, there your heart will be also." (Matthew 6:19–21)

■ **Thinking about heaven will bring peace—no matter how awful your circumstances here.**

You sympathized with those in prison and joyfully accepted the confiscation of your

property, because you knew that you yourselves had better and lasting possessions.
(Hebrews 10:34, NIV)

■ **Thinking about heaven, and its rewards, will shape
your priorities.**

Jesus said to him, "If you wish to be complete, go and sell your possessions and give
to the poor, and you will have treasure in
heaven; and come, follow Me."
(Matthew 19:21, NASB)

■ **Thinking about heaven's beauty gives you something
to look forward to.**

Then the angel showed me the river of the
water of life, as clear as crystal, flowing
from the throne of God and of the Lamb
down the middle of the great street of the
city. On each side of the river stood the tree
of life, bearing twelve crops of fruit…. And
the leaves of the tree are for the healing of
the nations.

There will be no more night. They will

not need the light of a lamp or the light of
the sun, for the Lord God will give them
light. (Revelation 22:1–2, 5, NIV)

■ **Thinking about heaven will keep you from making
money your goal.**

Command those who are rich in this present world not to be arrogant nor to put their
hope in wealth, which is so uncertain, but to
put their hope in God, who richly provides
us with everything for our enjoyment.
Command them to do good, to be rich in
good deeds, and to be generous and willing
to share. In this way they will lay up treasure for themselves as a firm foundation for
the coming age, so that they may take hold
of the life that is truly life.
(1 Timothy 6:17–19, NIV)

■ **Thinking about heaven can sustain you in the face of
great suffering or in the shadow of death.**

For I am already being poured out as a
drink offering, and the time of my depar-
ture is at hand.... And the Lord will deliver

me from every evil work and preserve me
for His heavenly kingdom.
(2 Timothy 4:6, 18)

What you love, Son, will control your
thoughts...and then your actions. I hope you will
make thinking about heaven a daily habit. It will lift
your gaze, and it will lift the whole focus of your life.

That is what I want for you. And that is my daily
prayer.

I've collected these words to leave you with
counsel and encouragement, "just in case I can't be
there." But if I can't be *here*, I will be *There*...in the
very presence of Jesus Christ...overflowing with
great joy...and waiting for you to join me.

Acknowledgments

First, let me say I am married to an amazing woman. She's very cute and sweet, but, more than that, she's the reason for the joy and blessing in our home. Joyce was always there when I couldn't be. I wanted her to know how thankful the boys and I are that she loves us.

This simple work was birthed out of a deep love I have for our sons. I wanted them to know my heart on a number of subjects. I also wanted the people who helped with this project to know my heart toward them. My great appreciation goes to Greg Dueker, Keith Reetz, Gayle Potter, and Debbie Matheny, who checked and rechecked references and read the manuscript with a helpful eye.

Thanks again and again to Larry Libby, my editor, for his touch upon my life. I feel humbled to be called his friend.